Discover Your Worth

Miriam Neff

This book is designed for your personal reading pleasure and profit. It is also designed for group study. A leader's guide with helps and hints for teachers and visual aids (Victor Multiuse Transparency Masters) is available from your local bookstore or from the publisher at $2.50.

VICTOR BOOKS

a division of SP Publications, Inc., Wheaton, Illinois
Offices also in Fullerton, California • Whitby, Ontario, Canada • London, England

The main Scripture version used is the *New American Standard Bible* (NASB), © 1960, 1962, 1968, 1971, 1972, 1973 by The Lockman Foundation, La Habra, California. Other quotations are from the King James Version (KJV); *The Living Bible* (LB), © Tyndale House Publishers, Wheaton, Ill.; *The Holy Bible: Revised Standard Version* (RSV), © 1946, 1952 by the Division of Christian Education of the National Council of the Churches of Christ in the United States; *New Testament in Modern English* by J. B. Phillips (PH), © 1958, The Macmillan Company. All quotations used by permission.

Second printing, 1979

Recommended Dewey Decimal Classification: 248.843
Suggested Subject heading: Woman

Library of Congress Catalog Card Number: 78-57953
ISBN: 0-88207-783-X

© 1979 by SP Publications, Inc. All rights reserved
Printed in the United States of America

VICTOR BOOKS
A division of SP Publications, Inc.
P.O. Box 1825, Wheaton, Illinois 60187

Contents

Preface 5
1. Love Stories Don't Just Happen 7
2. Search for Meaning 23
3. City of Refuge 37
4. Energy Unlimited 52
5. Blueprint for Oneness 67
6. Beyond Remodeling? 82
7. Marriage and Master Charge 94
8. Children: A Welcome Legacy 104
9. Reach Out 120
10. Planned Neglect 132
11. A Single Person 143
12. Who Is Equal? 159

Dedicated
to my husband,
Bob,
the most Christlike person I know.

My thanks to Mary Brown, Joanne Bowers, Karen Milonas, Bev Nelson, Margaret Nyman, Becky Shelton, Katie Warton, and Bonnie Miller. I am especially grateful to three women for being examples to me: Jean Good, Beulah Hinds, and Dorothy Neff.

Preface

A writer must have a purpose for writing. When she has four small children and a husband, purpose might be better called compelling desire. Otherwise the perspiration that accompanies inspiration would keep fledglings—like me—from completing page one.

Beyond the work of writing (yes, I said WORK) there is the agony of exposing your life and inner self to all who read your words. As long as a thought is hidden in my gray matter, I may consider it valid and of private worth. Putting it on paper bares my soul for criticism and evaluation from others. Equally painful is the exposure of my own life. For in order to speak to others about how God molds the clay of their lives, I need to tell how the Master Potter has so much to do as He works on me. I become vulnerable.

During the years that I have taught women's Bible studies, I have observed that many women are not aware of their potential. Feelings of inferiority and low self-esteem take over and prevent them from functioning at a fulfilling and joyful level.

Learning about women's roles, even about supposed scriptural roles, does not solve this problem. Rather, the solution lies in realizing how precious we are, as persons, as women, as uniquely ourselves, to the God who made us and continues to form us.

Acknowledging this value in ourselves frees us as women to function productively, happily, in whatever roles we fill—employee, wife, mother, friend, student, employer, grandmother, mother-in-law.

My purpose in writing is:

1. that you will discover your unique personhood through Jesus Christ

2. that you would let this knowledge free you in your relationships to others

3. that you will find in God's Word, the Bible, the source of your power and freedom and direction.

1.
Love Stories Don't Just Happen

I picked up the phone. The voice at the other end of the line sounded shaky. "Miriam, I'm scared. I don't trust myself. I'm afraid!" There was a pause broken by muffled sobs and stuttering. "I . . . I tried to take my life before . . . I don't know what I'll do . . . ."

"We will be right over," I assured her. In a few minutes when Bob and I pulled up in front of her house, Donna was sitting on her front steps with an overnight bag beside her. She looked as if she had aged five years in the past week. Her face was expressionless.

She got in the front seat with us. As darkness fell, we sped toward our home.

Our six-year-old Valerie wanted to lend her room to Donna for the night. Bubbling with the privilege of sharing with a guest, Valerie led her upstairs, pleased to have Donna's individual attention. She chattered about her dolls propped in corners, special wall-hangings and artwork. Donna's face began to show expression.

When our children were tucked in bed, Donna

and I sat down to talk. Twenty-five years of heartbreak spilled out—a fractured marriage in which four children grew to mistrust and fear their father. A second marriage in which Donna had tried to unite her new husband with four teenagers who were determined to lock him out of their lives. He might be her husband, but they would never accept him as father. She grew desperate from being confined with two warring forces, and loving both. The pressures that brought about her first attempt at suicide were evident, and were surfacing again.

Donna said that she felt she was a nobody. But I could see many successes in her life.

She said she saw herself as the ugliest of five girls in her family. To me she is an attractive woman with silver hair. She felt that she was dumb because she had dropped out of school to marry and does not have a college degree. But I knew she had done well in the courses she took.

Failure was all Donna could think about. Her successes were buried in her head. She felt as though she would never smile again. Why bother with tomorrow if it is going to be worse than today?

Donna had hardly eaten for days. As we snacked together, the hot tea seemed to soothe her frayed nerves. She talked about her feelings and then about her husband. Vitality began to color her placid expression. In our home there was no reminder of her past. She said she could not stand the pressure any more. I said she did not have to. She could stay with us.

She had said she could not do anything. I reminded her that she had raised four children and had held down a good job at the same time.

She said her husband did not love her. I told her

he was still with her. The cold war with the children had not driven him away.

The evidence mounted that maybe she wasn't a failure. She laughed. She said she was tired.

Donna had needed more than a listener. She needed evidence that tomorrow could be better. For Donna, at least there would be another day.

Broken Relationships

Donna is not alone. Divorce statistics (42 per 100 marriages) paint a dismal picture but that is only the tip of the iceberg. A prominent counselor has said that of the couples staying together, probably 50 percent are emotionally divorced.

Among North American women, depression is common, regardless of marital status. It usually stems from loneliness. Donna lived in a household of six people but felt utterly isolated. She communicated significantly with no one.

Brothers and sisters, after living together for years, may take great pains not to cross each others' paths as adults.

Hurt results from a relationship that is fractured but it is equally painful to discover you can build no lasting relationships. Most women say they have no "close" friends. Many say they don't need them. Not so. They may be unaware that they are diverting this need and satisfying it by vicariously living through their daughters, by becoming involved in soap-opera personalities, or even by substituting a bottle or food. The couple who are "best friends" is rare.

Four Cornerstones

God has a blueprint for relationships. They are to be based on Him for He is the Foundation. They are to be built by individuals committed to Him.

10 / Discover Your Worth

Why? Because that is part of God's blueprint.

There are four very important cornerstones that are vital in the structure of a joyful, fulfilling relationship. They are:

1. Acknowledgment of your own self-worth
2. Acknowledgment of another's self-worth
3. Communication
4. Making room

These cornerstones are not built overnight. But they are worth the commitment of time and involvement to establish them in your relationships, in your home, school, office, social groups, or church.

1. Acknowledgment of your own self-worth. I cannot overemphasize how important it is for a woman to have a healthy, positive self-concept. On what do we base our positive image of ourselves? On the fact that God created us. He does not specialize in inferior products. He formed us in our mothers' wombs. "For Thou didst form my inward parts; Thou didst weave me in my mother's womb. I will give thanks to Thee for I am fearfully and wonderfully made; wonderful are Thy works, and my soul knows it very well" (Ps. 139:13-14).

When God completed Creation and looked at all He had made, including woman, He saw that "it was very good" (Gen. 1:31).

That we were made by a caring God assures us of our worth. But we have an even more significant reason to love ourselves: God loves us. As we read through the Bible, we see that His love is unconditional. He has given us a complete Book filled with evidence of His love. I cannot comprehend that He loved me enough to give up His perfect Son for me. To exchange Jesus for Miriam goes beyond logic. That is called love. But God did it.

To see myself as inferior, now that Jesus has been exchanged for me, would be to devalue my loving Saviour.

Should this sense of my infinite worth make me proud? No. What is the source of my being? Who made me and gave me all I have? Who put me in the position I have? My Lord. I can take credit for nothing. But I do sense my value, and love the being God has created.

"But he who boasts, let him boast in the Lord. For not he who commends himself is approved, but whom the Lord commends" (2 Cor. 10:17-18). I see myself being stamped with this designation: Accepted Upon the Superior Recommendation of Jesus Christ.

What is the result of my positive self-image? I place myself under the Lordship of Jesus. I feed my spiritual being by reading God's Word and worshiping Him. I care for my physical body as a part of my stewardship. I protect my emotional being by entrusting it to my Lord and defending attacks against it with strength and security from His Word.

Does this consume all my time and attention? Definitely not. God did not place me here to exist in isolation, concentrating on self-preservation. In order to glorify Him I must reach out and serve others. But I can only do this by being secure of my personal worth.

Gail is 34. A family snapshot shows an attractive smiling woman sitting in a chair surrounded by three robust young children. As I talk with her I sense that here is a young woman with a positive outlook for the future and with faith in a personal caring God who has ordered the events of her life. Four years ago, Gail was run over by two Belgian

12 / Discover Your Worth

draft horses, each weighing a ton. Her spinal cord was severed. The result—she had no feeling from the waist down and would never walk again. Eight hospitalizations and many surgeries later, her condition is the same. Her husband crumpled under the shock. His way of coping was to leave.

Gail has always been a giving person. Before her third child was born, she was caring for two other children in addition to her own. Their mother was dying of cancer. Gail delighted in loving those children, even though her home was a small trailer.

Now she has learned the art of receiving. She says that when she becomes frustrated, when things are difficult, God reminds her of the many things she can do and the joys she shares, in His love, and with other people.

As Gail says, "Everyone is handicapped by things they can't do. I can't run or walk, but I can sew. I can comfort someone who physically hurts and mean it when I say, 'I know what you are going through.' And people believe me when I say, 'God cares and He will comfort you and give you His peace.'

"I do feel peace and I do believe that this is God's will for my life. His choice was for me to serve Him in a wheelchair in whatever ways He has for me—one of which is being a mother."

How can Gail still love her husband? Why does she always speak positively about him and encourage her children to respect him? Because she is secure in her own personal self-worth. She is also secure in God's dependable love. He has not rejected her because of the changes in her body. She accepts her paralysis. Recently she told me that one of her favorite verses is "And we know that all that happens to us is working for our good if we love

God and are fitting into His plans" (Rom. 8:28, LB).

In his excellent book, *How to Really Love Your Child,* Dr. Ross Campbell speaks of an emotional tank. This tank represents the emotional needs of the child. Campbell makes this statement: "Only if the emotional tank is full, can a child be expected to be at his best or do his best" (Wheaton, Ill.: Victor Books).

Here is the parallel. We are persons who need a sense of well-being, acceptance, and worth to function. God fills our tank with assurance of our worth to Him, acceptance, and love. Then we are able to function at peak capacity as He wants us to.

Today we are offered counterfeit means of keeping our tanks full. Our culture says all of these needs can be met without God. We can buy love; certain attractive physical characteristics will elicit acceptance from others. And since we are not spiritual beings, only "responders," we need no spiritual resources.

Advertising convinces us that all our needs can be satisfied through material channels, produced in the womb of technology, and brought into being by economic demand.

For example, the slogan for one new car is "Something to believe in." Can you imagine that slogan 10 years from now? There lies the once beautiful blue luxury model—now a rusted heap of bolts and scrap metal. Something to believe in?

"Passing the buck" is the most popular sport in our culture. People without God—and some who claim to know Him—see themselves as ultimately "not responsible," subject to their environment, powerless in the stream of life.

We live in a society in which psychology has

become a religion to many. Its systems are many, and whether the gurus are in flowing robe or gray flannel suit matters little.

Values are dispensed in American society via the media—magazines, newspapers, books, radio, movies and above all, television.

If we as Christians internalize those attitudes we will not be able to function. We will not glorify God. Our spiritual tanks will be empty. Our marriages will fail. Our parenting will falter. Our friendships will wane. Why? Because relating requires giving, and a person who lacks a sense of personal worth has nothing to give.

Worth does not come from things, or from systems, or from public consensus. Worth comes from God, and when we fill up on the realization of our worth to God, we can give. "Freely you received, freely give" (Matt. 10:8).

2. *Acknowledgment of another's self-worth.* We find through Scripture that our Creator is a God of balance. Were we to concentrate on our personal self-worth to the exclusion of the worth of others, relationships would become lopsided monsters, specializing in self-centeredness.

This is not God's intention. There is much in the Bible about seeing the worth of other people. All Scripture that applies to our personal creation applies to others as well. God was the Overseer when each one became a living soul, at the moment of conception. (See Psalm 139:13-14.)

God's love for my husband, for my child, for my friend, is infinite and unconditional. Since each one is such a special creation to God, can I view them with anything but high regard?

I am told to love my neighbor as myself (Matt. 19:19). But if I hold my husband and children in high regard and also am aware of my own personal worth, won't there be conflict?

No. Because of my awareness of our individual positions before God, the primary basis for conflict is removed. There is no power struggle when another person and I stand hand in hand on an equal plane before God. I have no need to win, to rule, to dominate. I am secure in my adequacy through my Lord. I have adequate resources from Him to give—to look out for the needs of others.

"Do nothing from selfishness or empty conceit, but with humility of mind let each of you regard one another as more important than himself; do not merely look out for your own personal interests, but also for the interests of others" (Phil. 2:3-4).

How do we behave when we recognize another's worth? Romans 12:10 gives us the answer: "Be devoted to one another in brotherly love; give preference to one another in honor."

Perhaps I can illustrate my point. We enjoy going out to breakfast as a family. Bob usually orders pancakes and enjoys them most with lots of butter. It gives me great pleasure to slip my butter onto his plate. It's one of my ways of honoring him.

The point is this: When we recognize another individual as a person of infinite worth to God, it affects how we treat him. We must internalize that we are *both* valuable to God before we can go to the third cornerstone.

3. *Communication.* We usually consider communication to be interaction at a verbal level: speaking. Actually, it is much broader than that. We convey messages through body language, neglected tasks, clothes we wear, food preferences, career, leisure activities, friends, and any number of other methods. In the broad sense, communica-

tion is any way that we convey information to other people.

We cannot consider communication in a Christian relationship without examining our inner nature. Ideally, communication would be relating our innermost thoughts and desires to the inner person of another.

In order to communicate with my husband, I need to be aware of what my inner being wants to say. Then I must convey it through my communication channel in such a way that he can pick it up accurately in his communication channel. Receiving my communication, he then interprets it in the light of his inner being. Realizing how complex communication is—and this is an oversimplified explanation—it is no wonder that our messages are often jumbled and we misunderstand each other!

Where do I learn to communicate? I begin with my inner being. There are two vital aspects that will determine whether I can communicate with my husband. They are (1) my positive image of myself and (2) my love for my husband, which becomes my channel.

We have already established that I must be assured of my worth to God before I can relate to anyone else. If I am negative about myself, everything I convey will be a question: "Am I worthwhile? Do you love me? Why don't you prove that I'm important?" We may tolerate this from a child, but we inwardly—if not outwardly—reject such messages from an adult, and especially a marriage partner.

Marcy was mothering her husband. He was oblivious to family expenses so she took care of all financial matters. He would ask her for his spending money. She couldn't understand his irresponsible money habits and did lots of worrying about notices for "insufficient funds."

When it came to questions regarding their family, whether it be purchasing a car or how to spend a holiday, Marcy stepped in and made the decision. She made "suggestions" to him non-stop about what he should do—and when and how.

There were periodic fights. When Dan's temper would snap, Marcy would play the martyr role. Dan would get his way (till he was pacified) and then Marcy would resume her old habits. Externally, Dan's display of temper was over something trivial. Internally, he was crying out, "Let me be a person. Let me think. Let me grow."

During one dispute, Dan said it was time to get a lawyer and determine the terms of divorce. Marcy was crushed. Of course, all the blame was put on Dan. It was his temper that was ruining their marriage, wasn't it?

Actually, Marcy was forever telling Dan what to do because she had a very low self-image. She was saying, "Help me feel that I'm important by answering my every whim." The message Dan got was "She's only looking out for herself." His response (this was unspoken): "I'll do things my way. I'm the head of this household." She got the message loud and clear. The result was that she felt more negative about herself. When Dan disregarded her directions and requests, she interpreted that as lack of love on his part. Were Dan and Marcy communicating? Of course not. Words were floating around between them under the same roof. But they certainly had little understanding of each other.

No matter how many communication tools we give to Marcy at this point, she will be ineffective.

She must accept herself as a person of worth before she can communicate with Dan.

Richard appeared to be the strong, silent type. Actually he was only silent. His wife felt he was aloof and cold. Their times together were *very* quiet. This couple could discuss their children's needs, their schedules, and household repairs, and that was about all. Richard could not open up and tell Sally about his dreams, hurts, or failures. Regardless of physical intimacy and living for years under the same roof, Sally felt that she was locked out of Richard's life. Why? Richard saw himself as a failure. Childhood experiences made him fear further rejection. He had a negative opinion of himself. He was afraid that if he really opened up with Sally, she would discover that he was a failure, and wouldn't accept the negative man inside.

He could not communicate. He had to first be assured that he, childhood experiences and all, was of infinite value to God, that he was a person of worth.

"The good man out of the good treasure of his heart brings forth what is good, and the evil man out of the evil treasure brings forth what is evil; for his mouth speaks from that which fills his heart" (Luke 6:45).

When two people are secure within themselves, they are ready to learn to communicate. Each partner has a channel through which he communicates. This channel is love and love is learned. Therefore, we can all acquire an adequate channel for communication.

When a married couple, a parent and child, or two friends establish between themselves a channel of love, they will experience much freedom in communication. When either person feels unloved he will react defensively to the other. He will be listening with one ear; the other will be saying, "What is she trying to get out of me?"

If the channel of love is missing we will be afraid to speak truthfully to each other. We are told in Ephesians 4:15 to speak the truth in love and to "grow up in all aspects into Him."

Maturing in communication means that we no longer need to wonder "how he will take it." We will know that our husband or friend is secure in our love and high esteem. What we say will not threaten him.

Does this mean we say whatever comes to our mind? No. Though we have a positive self-image and a loving channel of communication, we are not perfect. There are times when we feel like saying things that hurt. There are times when selfishness wins, and anger has the upper hand.

Our culture says, "Say whatever you feel like saying. Get it out of your system." What does Scripture say? "There is one who speaks rashly like the thrusts of a sword, but the tongue of the wise brings healing" (Prov. 12:18). "A gentle answer turns away wrath, but a harsh word stirs up anger. The tongue of the wise makes knowledge acceptable, but the mouth of fools spouts folly" (Prov. 15:1-2).

An important tool in communicating is eye contact. Whether you are speaking or listening, look into the eyes of the other person. We usually interpret lack of eye contact as disinterest. It is also evidence of low self-esteem. Establishing eye contact shows your mate that you are interested in what he is saying.

Eye contact helps you listen. Have you ever been involved in an "animated" conversation with your mate? With each statement you hear, you begin to determine how you're going to respond to that accusation. By the time you've organized that reply in your mind, your husband has gone on to the third topic and you missed the second one. We should not call that kind of conversation communication. One person is talking and the other person is thinking of what he'll say as soon as he can get a word in edgewise. Communication requires listening.

What most frequently prevents us from listening? Criticism. Why? We don't like what we're hearing so we tune out. Actually, those threatening moments can be most profitable. "Like an earring of gold and an ornament of fine gold is a wise reprover to a listening ear" (Prov. 25:12).

When we listen carefully, accepting criticism can become a profitable tool in communication. Our objective in listening to criticism is to determine whether we can learn from it and be a better person from what we've learned.

Communication is similar to exercising; it takes time and repeated efforts. There are many activities that Bob and I enjoy together that will probably be temporary. I doubt that we will be swimming, golfing, and hiking together when we're 80. However, I expect that we will still want to be intimately involved in each other's life.

For that reason, developing communication becomes a most vital part of our relationship. It is a high priority activity. Sometimes, the pace of our household prevents this vital part of our relationship. We have resorted to all sorts of special "plans" to have time to communicate. My favorite is to slip away for a weekend together. It sometimes takes half a day to get past the decisions that we need to make together. Then I can listen to what is happening in Bob's life.

That plan is rather complicated to pull off. So we have several alternatives. Plan B is to tuck the children in bed and call a neighborhood sitter to come do her homework at our house. We can then slip off to our favorite nearby spot for tea, or a sandwich, or whatever. Is it worth going out when you've both put in a full day? Yes, there's no laundry to fold, no phones to ring, and the waiter carries away the dirty dishes.

Plan C is used in desperation. We usually get up at 5:30. However, if we have a special book we want to read aloud together, or if we need to get in touch with each other, we set the alarm for 5:00 A.M. (You can imagine why I like Plan A best.)

It is worth the effort to communicate. Whatever the schedules ahead of us, we separate—knowing that we have the full support of the other, and that we are one in our marriedness, regardless of the differences in our worlds.

4. Making room. Our fourth cornerstone of relationships is making room. This means we make allowances for the faults or mistakes of others. Love requires this as a part of our behavior.

Some years ago, I wrote my personal paraphrase of 1 Corinthians 13:4–7. "I am very patient and kind, never jealous or envious, never boastful or proud, never haughty or selfish or rude. I do not demand my own way. I am not irritable or touchy. I do not hold grudges and will hardly even notice when my husband does me wrong. I am never glad about injustice, and rejoice whenever truth wins out. Because I love my husband (or child or friend) I will be loyal to him no matter what the cost. I will always stand my ground in defending him."

When we live these characteristics on a daily basis, we do not nitpick. Minor personal habits do not become a source of arguments. We give each other room to have different habits from our own. When the other fails, I see him through sympathetic eyes of love rather than an "I told you so" attitude. If he has a certain weakness, I protect him from criticism rather than expose his inability.

Many people think it is funny to cut down their mate or children. If you have a little humor, it's good for lots of laughs. But it isn't good for your relationships. Cutting down another person isn't "making room."

Have you developed the habit of being down on people, seeing weaknesses rather than strengths? Do you dwell on failures rather than another's abilities and potential? Read 1 Corinthians 13—the personalized version—every morning for a month or so. Memorize it. You will develop the ability to make room for your child, for your mate, for your friend.

2.
Search for Meaning

I had been employed for several years as a high school counselor. When I stopped working I felt a void. We were living in a large home and I had my own car. Our daughter, then one-and-one-half, required considerable care. Why did I feel frustrated? After nine months of searching for answers through "busy" shopping, poly-dome molding and painting, decoupage, and any number of other interests, I found the answer.

There was no paycheck made out to Miriam Neff. Before, at the end of every month, I could wave my little piece of paper showing in dollar amounts my worth. Now, there was no slip of paper. I was worthless!

It was painful to discover that my self-worth was determined by my bank account. I set out to discover another basis for my personal worth.

At that time in my life, I was stubborn, and had an inferiority complex submerged under a crust that said, "I can do all things through me if I work hard enough." I felt a tremendous sense of inadequacy in most situations, whether it was meeting a new person, making a comment in a group, or trying an unfamiliar sport.

To compensate for my low feelings of worth, I became a Yes person. Miriam would head 10 committees to gain approval. I very much wanted to conform to how "the group" did things.

Although I was outwardly a feminist, the idea of "freedom for women" had soured inside of me because I didn't even see many free, fulfilled men.

My Search Begins

My search for meaning began when I discovered my financial "worthlessness." Finding a solution, however, took far longer than this discovery. I felt fortunate to live in the 20th century. During many periods of history, women who wanted answers were not free to search, except within the narrow confines prescribed by their community.

We live in a literate society, with great resources available to us. We have time to study. Our minds and bodies need not concentrate on how to get enough food to survive another day. Most of us could be locked in our homes for weeks and still eat well.

I was already aware that my search was going to center on the Bible. I was, like so many people I know, affluent enough to own the Bible in several translations. Exploratory books are available to us. We have centuries of history on Christian living, and the biographies of men and women who have claimed God's promises and passed on to us a heritage of faith. We have the Holy Spirit to be our teacher. We have, by potential anyway, everything we need to be vital, growing Christians. But I didn't yet feel like I really possessed much of this.

Let Women Learn

Women have never had the opportunity for learning such as we have today. "Let women learn, with all quietness and due submission" (1 Tim. 2:11). We have dwelt too long on the "quietness and due submission" and need to underscore the "let women learn." We are free to study, to be educated, to work anywhere at almost anything, and to travel.

"From everyone who has been given much shall much be required" (Luke 12:48b). These words should be before us daily in our minds, if not in actual writing over our kitchen sink, by the makeup mirror, and in the front of our church sanctuaries or perhaps above the church door for all to see as we leave.

Are we taking advantage of our open doors? "That I may know Him" (Phil. 3:10) should be our goal. "So then each one of us shall give account of himself to God" (Rom. 14:12).

When I stand before God, there will be only one thing between God and me—what I have learned about God from the Scriptures. My husband will not be there to explain why I did or did not follow the Word. I cannot say, "Bob, tell God you didn't tell me what to do." I cannot say, "But, God, I couldn't launch out for You. I'm married and my husband might not have kept pace with me. That kind of initiative might have ruffled our marriage." "Therefore, to one who knows the right thing to do, and does not do it, to him it is sin" (James 4:17).

Motivations

As I began my search for meaning, I sensed that my privileges were accompanied by responsibility.

Responsibility is exciting. It means there are

goals to reach, strategy to lay, battles to fight, jobs to accomplish. I saw that my responsibility was accompanied by accountability. Accountability is equally exciting. It means reward and challenge. It provides motivation. I aim for perfection.

Undergirding all this action was the foundation of love. I was not motivated to act based only on a page, but by the person those words represent. I began to increasingly love the Person who created me, to know that He was vitally concerned with each day, and intensely interested in my success or failure.

With this motivation, the Bible became my searching ground. On what basis could I claim worth? Somehow it seemed that as I searched Scripture, I would discover that my husband was worth more than I. He was privileged to be born a man, you know. I was shocked to discover Psalm 139:15-16 (LB). "You were there while I was being formed in utter seclusion! You saw me before I was born and scheduled each day of my life before I began to breathe. Every day was recorded in Your Book!" Praise the Lord! I was not an accident. Neither was the fact that I was a woman! I read on: "How precious also are Thy thoughts to me, O God! How vast is the sum of them! If I should count them, they would outnumber the sand; when I awake, I am still with Thee" (Ps. 139:17-18).

I was important to God. The fact that He had plans for me proved that I was important to Him. I had not been living in this realization. But it was truth. A seed thought that took root in my mind would be responsible for many changes in my life. Searching the Bible was a worthwhile investment of time. A vague question that plagued me had been answered.

Can I Really Know God?

As I studied the same chapter, another question began to be resolved. My question had been this: with all my imperfections, can God and I have an intimate relationship?

I had been trying to define my relationships with God in terms of human associations. Friend accepts friend, based on what they have in common, or on what one can contribute to another. Relationships are rarely unconditional. In most relationships there is a point of diminishing returns: One has violated the other's trust. Mother has violated daughter's privacy. Mate has demanded beyond mate's endurance. Bound with these ideas of relationships I could not comprehend how God could become an integral, permanent, satisfying part of my world.

Nor could I imagine that I could be used by Him for anything really special. The words of Psalm 139 filtered through my mind. "Where can I go from Thy Spirit? Or where can I flee from Thy presence? If I ascend to heaven, Thou art there, if I make my bed in Sheol, behold, Thou art there" (vv. 7-8). I was not out of God's reach during those dark periods.

"If I take the wings of the dawn, if I dwell in the remotest part of the sea, even there Thy hand will lead me, and Thy right hand will lay hold of me" (vv. 9-10). In the most beautiful days and during the most unusual or lonely experience, I was still His child. Verse 6 expressed my wonder: "Such knowledge is too wonderful for me; it is too high, I cannot attain to it."

While pursuing God for answers, I saw that He could search me. I made verses 23 and 24 my prayer. "Search me, O God, and know my heart:

try me, and know my anxious thoughts; and see if there be any hurtful way in me, and lead me in the everlasting way." It was a bold request and God took me up on it!

To delve for worth in God was an exciting challenge. I determined to get to know Him intimately.

Daily Discipline

The Bible grew in importance in my life until my daily therapy was reading Scripture. Strange how I had never "had time" before. Now, little blocks of time popped up here and there: early mornings, children's naptimes, evenings when my husband traveled.

Daily Bible reading was not, however, a "happily ever after" story. Our family grew. Quiet moments at the Neff residence were rare. When it looked like there was hope for some quiet moments, the phone jangled. God confirmed to my heart that I needed to get up earlier, ahead of the crowd. But surely, He would not expect that of me? He did not create me to be a "morning" person. I did not even have a robe to wear for the occasion!

My husband turned the alarm back. He was a morning person. He would help me. How peaceful it was to read in the dusky light of sunrise. I could never read enough to satisfy my heart before little feet could be heard on the stairs. Our children knew that those minutes were precious and that there was an aura in the early quiet time that was not sensed in the hustle of the day. But read on we would, peering at our Bibles over tousled heads cuddled in our laps. We found that consistent Bible study does not happen without discipline. As Dr. Warren Wiersbe has said, "Sometimes the most spiritual thing you can do in a day is roll out of bed and reach for your Bible." That may be your biggest battle on some days.

"Reverence for God adds hours to each day" (Prov. 10:27, LB). He can make you feel those hours were added during the night when you make room for Him in your day.

"The joy of the Lord is your strength" (Neh. 8:10). Some people have revised that to: "Eight hours of sleep shall be your strength." The joy of the Lord gives us more zest for living than sleep. And what greater source of joy than God's Word!

A girl once told me that she never failed to read the Bible before she went to work, but she did not find it necessary when she stayed home. I do not think sin and the forces of evil know the difference! Bitterness, envy, lusts of flesh, and selfishness feel at home either place. The woman who enters the working world daily does have special temptations the woman at home might not face as frequently. To many men, any woman is viewed with lust, and a wedding band does not provide a barrier. She may be propositioned within circumstances that provide ample room for sin. If she is surrounded with women who do not consider God's standard of any regard, peer pressure increases.

One nurse became involved with a married doctor with whom she worked daily. Though she was a Christian she could not muster the courage to say No. She was reminded of Romans 13:14. "But put on the Lord Jesus Christ and make no provision for the flesh in regard to its lusts." Their working relationship provided ample "provision for the flesh." One solution seemed clear. Stop working at that hospital. Drastic? Yes, perhaps. She took that step. It was not easy. One reward that she began to enjoy immediately was freedom from the heaviness of guilt. She had not realized how heavy that weight had become in her life.

An emotional scar remains from that period of her life. We read in the Bible, "No other sin affects the body as this one does" (1 Cor. 6:18, LB). The scar, however, is covered over with forgiveness and is a reminder of God's grace. The one who is forgiven much, loves much (Luke 7:47).

It is accurate to say that a woman needs time in the Bible before daily entering the working world, and a woman in the home needs the same preparation. Irritability, due to constant care of children, idleness, and anger, comes in stealthily. Soap operas and self-pity can clutter our minds. In my early morning reading time, verses jump off the page that answer my current problem.

David provided us with a method to claim more power from God's Word. "Thy Word have I treasured in my heart, that I may not sin against Thee" (Ps. 119:11). When a verse does answer a problem, I write it on a recipe card to memorize during that day. That card can be propped by the kitchen sink, pinned above my sewing machine, slipped into a sweater pocket while I am outside with the children, or clipped to the handlebars of my bike. During the day, I review the verse and soon it is "treasured in my heart."

When I am ready to explode at a child and my Bible is out of arms reach, as it usually is when I am tempted to sin, God speaks through His Word, "Let everyone be quick to hear, slow to speak, and slow to anger" (James 1:19). Or, when I am beginning to dwell on some fault of one of my Christian brothers or sisters, Philippians 4:8 comes to mind: "Finally, brethren, whatever is true, whatever is honorable, whatever is right, whatever is pure, whatever is lovely, whatever is of good repute, if there is any excellence and if anything worthy of praise, let your mind dwell on these things."

Will I ever be completely free of feelings of anger or bitterness? No. It's part of my old nature, and I'll not be completely free of it till I'm with the Lord. However, I do not have to let my old nature dictate my behavior.

This, for me, is taking "the sword of the Spirit, which is the Word of God" (Eph. 6:17). The Word of God activates more of God's transforming power than any other source.

How Do You Change Behavior?

As a high school counselor I worked with many students who had problems. Some were seen regularly by psychologists or other specialists. A few spent time in hospitals with the objective of breaking habits and changing thought patterns. Sometimes there were positive changes. Often these changes were temporary. I never saw dramatic transformations resulting from the professional counseling.

Carie was 18. In the last few years her parents had spent $30,000 for professional help for her. Today she is unhappy, unmarried, pregnant, and dependent on her parents, though she openly states she can't stand them. There has been no permanent benefit from all the "help" she received. She is still a chronic liar, still threatening to take her own life. She sees nothing optimistic in the future.

Studies in learning show us that habit is a complex part of human behavior and is not easily changed. We may change behavior in a new environment, but what happens when the person goes home?

God is a transformation specialist. He is a renewer of minds. He loves us to use His Word to free us from problems that confine us. Our fuzzy concerns become clarified.

In the middle of our concerns and confusions we pick up our Bibles and begin to read. As we let His knowledge filter through our minds, His priorities for us sort through the confusion. Sometimes specific problems are made clear or answered; if not, we still find a calm that puts our concerns in perspective.

As I studied the Bible more intensely, I found that it had radical solutions to problems, not heavy, stiff casts to cover up wounds. God's solutions were psychologically sound. I saw the Bible as a valuable textbook as well as a source of inspiration. My commitment to the Bible, as a source book for successful daily living, grew.

The Bible Versus Society

In the Bible, I saw a study in contrasts to the world and society in which I had been operating. Women were clamoring for their freedoms to be legislated. I saw that the Bible says the law cannot guarantee freedom (John 8:32-36). Many women refuse to be bound to the job of child-rearing, considering children a nuisance to be avoided. The National Women's Conference recommends federal initiative for comprehensive, voluntary child-care centers. The Word says, "Children are a gift of the Lord" (Ps. 127:3a).

Marriage vows are changed from sacred promises to statements of what each wants to gain from the union. "It would be impossible for us to attain our ideal if we did not build individual freedom into our union. At the acknowledged risk of separation we must be true to ourselves as we are now, and as we come to be. We must continue to explore and expand as persons, in order to grow as mates" (Howard Kirschenbaum and Rockwell Stensrud, *The Wedding Book*. New York; Seabury Press). This marriage ceremony sounds like two individuals' declaration of independence. God's Word says that two become one. This does not sound so individualistic!

Ads in women's magazines and on television picture the successful woman as a lawyer, beautiful, slim, young, vigorous. She has, at most, two self-sufficient children, and a husband may or may not be in the picture. If he is, he certainly does not interfere with her career!

Many women who have chosen not to be gainfully employed have not come up with a satisfactory solution to using the hours of the day. With countless appliances to help them do the housework there is an excess of time. Wandering through shopping centers, charge cards in hand, and going "out to lunch" becomes a pastime to tire the feet but leave the mind empty. An empty mind provides an open door for the excitement of the soap operas or an affair on the side.

Sara thought that greater emotional involvement would help fill her days. But after she had heard her neighbors' problems and had searched for more varied friendships, the void was still there.

A woman needs purpose, a sense that her activities are worthwhile, and that she—in her work as well as in her person—commands the respect of her family and friends.

Feelings of Inferiority

As I studied women, I realized that many were plagued with feelings of inferiority. Donna was. By wanting to take her own life she was making a statement about herself. "I am worth so little, I should not exist."

Low feelings of self-worth say, "God, You made an inferior product in creating me. You do not have the power to transform me into something worthwhile, something beautiful." That attitude blocks God's power out of our lives.

Fear

Fear runs the lives of many women. Linda was afraid to drive—ever since the day that a sudden sense of desperation came over her while she was in the middle of city traffic. Frantic and perspiring profusely, she was unable to decide whether to go when the light changed or to jump from her car and run and hide.

This is a type of agoraphobia, or an abnormal fear of crossing or of being in open spaces. This fear plagues many people. However, attaching an impressive name to her fear did not lessen Linda's suffering. She was determined never to sit behind the steering wheel again.

Fear was restricting her life. Job possibilities were reduced to places she could reach on bus routes. What could be done?

Fortunately, Linda's story *was* rather than *is*. After years of living with her fear, she decided to trust God to help her do what she could not do alone. Scripture is full of instructions on conquering fear. "There is no fear in love; but perfect love casts out fear, because fear involves punishment, and the one who fears is not perfected in love" (1 John 4:18).

Linda began to memorize Scriptures about fear. She put verses in the car to review. She began to drive short distances with someone at her side. Today, she is driving without fear.

Another woman who lived alone said that she could not free herself from fear at night. I suggested to her that she memorize a few verses that she found especially meaningful. Then, when she began to feel fearful she could consciously review them. She did this and found herself praising the Lord.

Strength in Crisis

During the Viet Nam conflict some men who were in prison shared Scripture with each other. It kept them sane and caused other prisoners to accept Christ. There are many accounts in history of God's people confined in prison and enduring suffering, and yet experiencing freedom of mind and heart because because of the Scripture they had memorized.

It seems unlikely that many Christians today will be forcibly prevented from reading their Bibles. But were it to happen, would we starve spiritually? God needs women today who are learning. He uses His resources wisely. You can be sure that when you begin to memorize Scripture it will be used.

I had just learned that my mother had cancer. To summarize Mama's life in one sentence: She was the most giving, selfless woman I have ever known. I wrestled with the possibility that God might soon end her giving on this earth.

A few days later, I was directed to memorize 1 Thessalonians 4:13-18, verses telling of the

Christian hope of resurrection after death, and of life eternal with God and with loved ones. It comforted me to concentrate on the fact that Mama would delight in the presence of her Lord. I also could rejoice that she and I would meet in heaven someday and our relationship would begin again at a different level. I drew strength from those verses during those days of facing reality.

In that same week a friend's mother took her own life. My friend wept outwardly, but inwardly she was angry and full of hate. Why did her mother choose that method to "get even" with the family? Her heart cried, "Why me? Wasn't I a good enough daughter to make my mother's life worthwhile?" I had words of comfort from Scripture, but my friend did not. Jesus is not her Lord.

As we knelt together at her mother's casket, only I could pray. My friend could only grieve. My burden for friends who did not know Christ grew that day. Later, as I pulled my boys around the neighborhood in their wagon, I looked at the homes of my friends and resolved to be a more vocal and living epistle of my Lord. I began carrying out God's marching orders that I had formerly relegated to Bible classes but not to my neighborhood. "Wherefore comfort one another with these words" (1 Thes. 4:18, KJV) had fresh meaning that day.

I began to grasp in a small way that the truth that was revolutionizing my life could not be contained. Scripture that was freeing me from fear, indecision, and inferiority would filter out from me.

It was like being in a stuffy closed room and opening a lakeside window to let fresh invigorating winds change the whole room. God's truth and its effects would go with me wherever I went, and sweep through every relationship.

3.
City of Refuge

Our traditional ideas of a family center on a Thanksgiving Day in the country. Grandparents, parents, and children gather around a turkey. Grandmother smiles as her adult children, who have come in from their nearby farms, admire her culinary talents. The children snitch pinches from the shell of the pumpkin pie.

Our concepts of home have changed with the years. My family includes no farmers by trade, though Papa is still one at heart. My sisters and I drive four to six hours each way to gather at "the homestead," our parents' third home since they left the farm. None of us have ever lived in the present home, so it seems like a house and not a home. Food is there, but it is not the center of attention. The rare occurrence of being together is the central attraction.

What is the bond that makes us drive many miles to be together? It certainly is not the ease of the drive to get there; several hours in a car with small children is surely not ease. The drawing force is that we are a family.

What Is "Family"?

That term means little to many people today. Children migrate or are transferred to different parts of the United States or beyond, and reunions become a major expense. Ties that were shaky when everyone was under one roof become nonexistent when there are many miles of separation. Parents split and it becomes awkward to get the "family" together. Children find it easier to forget family than to work through the conflicts of being accepted. They fear that the individual they have become will no longer fit in their family niche. Family, as a reality, becomes a fuzzy concept.

Janet doesn't look forward to family get-togethers. Her husband, Roger, can no longer stand his brother. If he can find no excuse to miss the family gathering, he at least finds a remote room and isolates himself from the group.

Roger feels his brother is at fault. The entire atmosphere is affected by the electric tension between these brothers. Roger and his brother never built a relationship.

Children learn devastating lessons from such examples: Hold onto your grudges selfishly. Never mind the hurts they cause. Being a family means nothing. "I" am what matters.

Family Places

Behind the memories of family there is a place where roots took hold. The place in itself is not important but, strangely enough, boards and plaster, cement and brick take on meaning. The Bible has relatively little to say about earthly homes. They appear only as a backdrop for building relationships.

When God sent Abraham to the land He had given him, Abraham pitched his tent between two mountains, Bethel and Ai. *Bethel* means "house of God" while *Ai* means "a heap of ruins." What a contrast! Our homes fall somewhere on a continuum in between. Unfortunately, a home that externally appears to be the house of God can be dangerously close to disaster and turn to a heap of ruins within months or even weeks. What a challenge to achieve a home that God can dwell in! This place where relationships are formed is to be founded on one vertical relationship—with the Lord. When our relationship with the Lord is firm, we can then teach our children of Him (Deut. 4:9–10; 11:19).

The house where all this takes place can be as varied as each unique union of man and wife. But the function of teaching about the Lord and growing with Him remains the same. Our homes will approach being a house of God only to the extent that we fulfill His instructions. How the devil delights in *things* taking precedence over *people*. If he can divert our attention to the pictures in magazines of how the ideal home should look, he has gained considerable headway.

A Perfect Place?

Advertising today presents a home as being many beautiful rooms without real people in them. No wonder the floors are white and there is no traffic pattern in the lush carpeting. The newspaper stays folded in its rack, the beverage cups gleam with no crumpled napkins in them. There are no bathtub rings, and all the plants are vigorous and green. There is nothing wrong with all that neatness and beauty unless we work to achieve that as our objective rather than to provide a shelter where living and growing can take place.

We visited such a home once. All children were ushered to a separate territory. If they entered the "adult" area to be reassured of their parents' presence, they were watched with a nervous gaze. The aura of the home cried out, "Look at these lovely things." I wondered if the children ever yelled back, "I live here too!"

A Growing Place

A home should provide a place where parents, children, and houseguests can take risks in exploring that which would be threatening anywhere else. Sitting down at a piano to "compose" might be laughed at in the school music room, but home is a safe place to try new sounds and rhythms. New art objects can be shaped, chalked, carved at home—creations that would not emerge under critical eyes in the classroom. A quiet corner can be found for thinking or resting after the traffic jams of the day. The rooms of the home are where husband, wife, and children grow. "By wisdom a house is built, and by understanding it is established; and by knowledge the rooms are filled with all precious and pleasant riches" (Prov. 24:3-4).

I look forward to going to the place which Jesus is preparing for me (John 14:2). The fact that He is preparing it for me makes this place a delight to anticipate. Whatever my need, it will be provided for there. I hope I can achieve a slight parallel to that in our home. Can my husband anticipate that he will come home to a place prepared for him? Do my children know that when they walk in the door after school or play, I will be ready for them? Is our home prepared for them or for the eyes of a critical neighbor? Can I hurry there after harrowing activities and know that a calm will envelop me as I open the door and I enter my front hall?

Place of Refuge

In the Old Testament, cities of refuge were established for people to run to when they were falsely pursued for murder. If they reached one of these cities, the crime could not be avenged as long as they were there.

Women are the keepers of the home, builders of a place of refuge. Women today spend much time, worry, and money on the physical aspects of a home and its upkeep. In fact, the physical home and its "preservation" often upstages the main function: that of being a backdrop for building relationships, the primary relationship being one with God.

In our homes, emotional well-being should be nurtured, not shattered. Hurts from the day heal in the perspective of being accepted. Reactions can be explored in the light of God's standard. This is a far cry from what many homes have become. For many couples, the home itself is the cause for bickering and heated arguments. It is the center of a power struggle, a place to vent frustrations.

I talked with an insecure student after school one day. It always took him great amounts of time to make decisions and we were trying to decide on his next schedule of classes. He wanted me to meet his mother, so after our session I took him to his house. His mother was unaware that I had entered the home when she heard her son close the front door. A torrent of criticism came from the kitchen, interspersed with curses. No wonder he was insecure. In his own home he was belittled and degraded. I learned more about this student in those five minutes than in hours of counseling at school.

Calculate the Cost

One cause for friction in homes is the fact that home and its expenses are beyond the couple's income. "Prepare your work outside, and make it ready for yourself in the field. Afterwards, then, build your house" (Prov. 24:27). This is a wise principle to follow today. Get established in your work and then choose your home according to your income. Many young couples dreamily search for a place where they can be happy, and they sign a contract before they have calculated the cost of payments and upkeep.

Attractive surroundings do not compensate for the tension of bank overdrafts. Husbands feel pressured to increase the income and take second jobs or positions for which they are unsuited. This brings more pressures and family tension. A root feeling grows in them that they are valued in proportion to the size of their paycheck.

People fade into the background and things take priority. The household moves toward Mount Ai. "The wise woman builds her house, but the foolish tears it down with her own hands" (Prov. 14:1). Intentionally? Probably not.

It is so easy, even natural, to drift with the majority rather than to search God's Word and in His wisdom build our house. To gain wisdom to build our house we must go to the source of wisdom. Psalm 111:10 tells us: "The fear of the Lord is the beginning of wisdom: a good understanding have all they that do His commandments."

We find much in Scripture to help us in household management. Our willingness to obey allows and invites God to open our minds to understand what we read. Then, as we apply those things we are able to understand more, and so we grow.

A Wise Woman

In the last chapter of Proverbs, we are shown a picture of an unusual woman. This story gives us many insights into the great task a woman has in building a house of refuge for her family. There is great variety in the task and no suggestion of molds into which women must be cast. The job God gives to each woman will be as individual as the uniqueness He created into her being. An all-wise God who is intensely interested in our welfare does not fill us with gifts, abilities, energy, and drives, and then confine them all to strict conformity.

A second insight we gain is that more is said about the wise woman's personal characteristics than her activities. In Proverbs 31:10-31, 13 verses refer to the woman's character and 9 refer to specific activities. Our activities are important, but they will be empty if they are not based on transformed personal characteristics.

Looking at her personal profile we see that the characteristics she possessed are just as rare today as they were in her time. The profile would include a summary like this: trustworthy, good, positive self-image, asset to her husband, optimistic, wise and kind, industrious, highly respected by her family, excellent, generous, good reputation, loves the Lord, and prepared for whatever action God sends her way.

If we could acquire those characteristics, would we automatically be able to manage our households and other jobs? I doubt it. Just as we must learn these characteristics from God, we must learn the "how to" of the activities. Our formula for learning is found in Titus 2: Older women teach younger women. Some mothers are able to teach their daughters. But in our mobile society many mothers are not accessible when daughters need help and teaching regarding their families. It is helpful to find an older, mature Christian woman, perhaps in your local church, on whom you can lean on for advice.

My mother taught me the "how to's" of spring, fall, and post-Christmas cleaning. The procedure involved dismantling the whole house and scrubbing everything. Today, that does not suit the needs of our household. Deep-cleaning one room a month so that each room gets cleaned once a year is enough. Our home is always "together" and ready to be shared and used. My method would not work in my mother's coal-heated home where periodic "explosions" of the furnace would leave a film of black over everything and a delivery of coal to the cellar meant a sooty cloud would fill our home as shovel after shovel was added to the bin. I learned, however, that cleaning was a part of being a keeper of the home. Neat surroundings encourage a positive self-image. Looking well to the ways of her household is one evidence of godliness visible to people and part of a woman's testimony.

Clothing

The virtuous woman in Proverbs 31 was not concerned about cold weather. Her family was prepared with suitable clothing for any season. That requires foresight and sometimes sacrificing our present wants for future needs. However, for most people in the United States, lack of clothing is not a common problem. Our overstuffed closets should weigh heavily on our consciences in the light of need in many parts of the world. Job 27:16 illustrates that excessive changes of clothing are a characteristic of the godless. This is repeated in the New Testament.

"And why are you anxious about clothing? Observe how the lilies of the field grow, they do not toil nor do they spin. Do not be anxious then, saying, 'What shall we eat?' or 'What shall we drink?' or 'With what shall we clothe ourselves?' For all these things the Gentiles eagerly seek; for your Heavenly Father knows that you need all these things. But seek first His kingdom and His righteousness; and all these things shall be added to you" (Matt. 6:28, 31-33).

Balance is our objective. We should not be outlandish in either extreme. A key to this is realizing that our clothing is part of our stewardship. Everything belongs to Him. This gives us added incentive to take care of things properly. God will not ask us what brand of clothing our children have worn or which dress shops we frequented. Habitual window-shopping to keep abreast of latest fashion trends is not an obligation. Giving too much attention to clothes robs us of time we could be using more wisely.

I once thought that sewing for the needy was only for centuries past and that Dorcas would have been given a different gift today, one more appropriate for our times. I was wrong. A friend and I were en route downtown when she spotted a beautiful, expensive dress in a window. We looked and went on; anything in that shop was beyond our combined pocketbooks.

I closeted myself in my sewing room shortly afterward and the idea came to create my own version of that dress for my friend. The following Sunday I slipped the box containing my creation under her arm. As she folded back the tissue her tears of joy brought my tears too. She had been battling self-pity over financial sacrifices she had needed to make for her family. The Lord knew her need and guided me—via my machine—to create a dress that fit her perfectly.

Food

The virtuous woman takes responsibility for preparing food for her family. With all her involvement, no wonder she rises before the sun does. She is "not lagging behind in diligence" (Rom. 12:11). Those in her household receive their portion. Quantity in our country is not a problem, but quality is. Realizing that our bodies belong to the Lord, we will eat what is good for them. Stewardship means children who have had a nutritious breakfast—after enough sleep—and who can concentrate on studying at school; or men and women who can be industrious without midmorning slumps. "Why do you spend money for what is not bread, and your wages for what does not satisfy? Listen carefully to Me, and eat what is good, and delight yourself in abundance" (Isa. 55:2).

When Saul's men needed quick energy, God gave

them honey. It was exactly what they needed, but they refused to eat it. As a result, they later ate the wrong thing (1 Sam. 14:24-35). Giving our children a steady diet of convenience foods would be like God giving Saul's men cotton candy to restore their strength. Eating is a lifetime requirement. What we eat determines our health, our energy, and sometimes our moods. We should learn what is good for us and change our habits.

Add together the time you spend grocery shopping, cooking, and washing dishes. Can you imagine how much of your total life is spent around food? That makes it worth doing a time study on the topic to see where you can save minutes. In a week you may save several hours. After we studied our own household, we changed several habits. We grocery shop once a month. I make double batches of most main dishes and desserts, one to be used now and one for the freezer or someone else. Time over the stove or mixer is also time for children to taste, help, and jabber. Feeding the family is not an ogre that monopolizes my weekly calender.

At one time I thought living in the city was a drain on our grocery budget. Friends with more sunny space filled their tables and freezers with home-grown green beans, corn, and *real* tomatoes. After searching and listening to budget-conscious city dwellers I found that I had advantages too. We have discount frozen food stores, bakery outlets, farmers' markets and discount food chains.

Verses 8 and 9 of Proverbs 30 help me keep the kitchen demands in perspective. "Feed me with the food that is my portion, lest I be full and deny Thee and say, 'Who is the Lord?' or lest I be in want, and steal, and profane the name of my God." God gave us our bodies on loan. While we should not ignore their needs, neither should we spend inordinate amounts of time and money to satisfy physical needs.

The woman in Proverbs had servant girls. It was her responsibility to see to it that the household chores got done; she did not have to do them all herself. No wonder she was optimistic. She felt the fulfillment of being productive and creative. There was no room for boredom in her schedule.

"She girds herself with strength" (v. 17a). The girdle at that time was used to keep clothes out of the way, freeing a woman for moving and working. She was prepared for action. In Scripture, the word *girdle* was often used in a figurative sense, as it is here, as a symbol of power, strength, and activity. 1 Peter 1:13 says, "Gird your minds for action."

Career Woman

The virtuous woman in Proverbs 31 would today be classified as a working woman. While we are instructed to be keepers at home, that does not always take 24 hours a day. Work expands to fill whatever time it can devour. Why not confine it to the least number of hours possible and tackle a new project? Today, this virtuous woman might have been a realtor, gardener, weaver, or garment designer and distributor. She would also qualify as a personnel supervisor or management consultant. This was done without neglecting or alienating her family.

Christian women who opt to work face the challenge of finding a satisfying job that does not compete with home and family. We do not have the option to disregard the heritage from God of our children and husbands. We do not have the option of burying our gifts in the sand, either. One advantage we have is that our society is full of variety in work possibilities. A woman can have her own business, work projects can be done in the home, and some school systems have variable schedules. We can use this flexibility to advantage.

When You Have to Work

In our society, we see an increasing number of women who must work, to provide part or all of the family income. Such a woman must be careful to order her priorities. A common mistake is to believe that you can add a full work day to your present activities. I have not discovered one woman who is physically and emotionally able to do this. Fatigue gnaws on frayed nerves and a sense of "things will never get better" or "I'll never catch up" moves in like a dark cloud.

Remember that you needn't do things the same way year after year. Cleaning, cooking, mending, and community involvement all need adjusting to fit in to what is possible. And while family members should take responsibility to share in household work, they don't always. Sometimes it is better to let certain tasks go undone till other members assume them than to work and nag and add strained relationships to your list of problems.

The woman who works full-time must be careful not to neglect the people in her life. Food, cleaning, clothes, and schedules can easily fill every nonworking hour. But relationships can't be replaced. Time with each child, friend, or time with your husband must be guarded even if it means skipping something else.

Our city of refuge is where we're molding eternal beings—people. They learn there that Christ is their "forever" city of refuge. Because of our sin, we can escape to Him. In the Old Testament, a person stayed safely at the city of refuge till the high priest of that city died. Our High Priest, Jesus Christ, will never die, and so our refuge is permanent. Children must sense the security of their city of refuge, regardless of Mother's work schedule.

The Hours of My Day

We do not know what God will put in a day. I had a friend who was unemployed for several weeks. My home was a handy stopping-off spot between job interviews. There was always coffee, the bustle of children, and conversation there. I prayed that in her visits she would see Jesus in my life; not Jesus, the good man that she knew, but Jesus, my personal, risen Lord who deserves total commitment. Day after day the laundry collected and the dust shifted as we talked about her past job, family, and interviews. I finally prayed one morning, "Lord, don't let her come today. I've got to catch up, and besides, *my* objective is not happening."

The doorbell rang at 9 A.M. "But, God, I told You." She stood there smiling. She had only a little time before interviews. "Thank You, Lord." That morning we talked of Jesus and the fact that such a good Man deserved the right to be heard. We discussed what He said about heaven and hell, what He said about Himself, and what He wanted His followers to do. My hours of listening were not wasted; now it was my turn to speak. Also, I learned a lesson about being prepared for action God sends my way. My light is not to be turned on and off like a welcome mat that is spread out when *I* feel like sharing. God sees the overall view infinitely better than I do. Why should not He direct the traffic on my doorstep? It seemed the pile of laundry disappeared faster and the dust too, as I flew around working and delighting in the fact that God let me, an unpolished recruit, be in on His battle.

Your House Is God's House

The virtuous woman of Proverbs 31 reached out her hands to the poor and needy. It is easy to give out of our abundance, but it is also good to give when our resources are skimpy.

My kitchen appliances and pantry are God's. My washing machine is His. When it stops working I talk to Him about it before calling the repairman. More than once I have cancelled a repairman's visit because "God who made the world and all things in it" (Acts 17:24) has intervened for some sick appliance or pipe. He does not need to do that to prove to me His ability. I believe He is able regardless, but how graciously He intervenes anyway.

The virtuous woman received praise for her good deeds. What reaction have we earned as a fruit of our hands? Perhaps none. I want to be worthy of praise, but that is not my motivation for action.

I work to make a home, a house of refuge for my loved ones. I act to obey and to please my Lord. Then, whether or not I receive any thanks or praise is irrelevant, because someday I will hear, "Well done . . . you were faithful with a few things, I will put you in charge of many things: enter thou into the joy of your Master" (Matt. 25:23).

4.
Energy Unlimited

You don't want to be God's caterpillar if He designs you to be His butterfly. Why crawl along confined in space, conforming to the surrounding colors, if you can be a breathtaking contrast to your world? If you can fly?

Before you can emerge from the cocoon, you must internalize some mind-boggling facts. You can't escape confinement till you see the intimate relationship God has planned for you through prayer.

"We have the mind of Christ" (1 Cor. 2:16). "No longer do I call you slaves; for the slave does not know what his master is doing; but I have called you friends, for all things that I have heard from My Father I have made known to you" (John 15:15).

Can you grasp that you are the special friend of God's Son? That He wants you to know His mind and thoughts? In fact, He has provided a channel for this transfer of wisdom, the Holy Spirit (John 16:13-15).

Do you understand that you can communicate with God? "Call to Me, and I will answer you, and

I will tell you great and mighty things, which you do not know" (Jer. 33:3).

Can you believe that you influence God by your requests? "If you abide in Me, and My words abide in you, ask whatever you wish, and it shall be done for you" (John 15:7).

What Is Prayer?

How can a perfect God permit and even want us to have this kind of relationship with Him? How can we immerse ourselves in that relationship and enjoy it to the fullest?

Remember, we were made in His image and likeness. We were made to fill, subdue, and have dominion over the earth and everything in it. We are to be God's representatives on earth. It is logical that as God's vice-regents, we would need constant communication with Him in order to accomplish what He wants done. This is what prayer is.

If you were to conduct a survey about prayer, you would hear a majority of the people you ask say that they have prayed some time in their lives, perhaps even often. But if you changed the subject to effective prayer as described in the Bible, that majority would quickly diminish.

A mother of four called me one night. She was depressed and she cried as she talked. She couldn't understand why God was not answering her prayer and lifting the smothering cloud around her. The longer she talked, the more some revealing facts began to surface. It was her habit to spend a lot of time on the phone. Her home was cluttered and unkept. She felt that children's baths were her husband's responsibility to supervise. If he didn't do it, it wasn't done. Picking up toys on the lawn, raking and all other outdoor work was his also. Looking around her home became a depressing experience!

We women are told to be keepers of the home. She had some obeying to do. It is not easy to methodically begin cleaning house when you don't feel like it. But that's obedience. As she obeyed the cloud began to lift for her.

Have *you* wondered why God hasn't answered a prayer of yours? What is prayer? How does it become integrated into daily life?

Acceptance of Christ

The fact that God created all people does not make each of us His personal child. That's His desire, but we see from 1 John 2:23 that we cannot have Him as Father without acknowledging Jesus as His Son. Many cries of "Oh, God" are not heard simply because the individual has not acknowledged Jesus. I have a friend in that position. She prays, but as for accepting Jesus, her answer is "Not yet." It is obvious that God has not unleashed His power in her life. Yes, spring rain falls on both sides of the street and her home is warm in winter as is mine. In some material aspects, our lives are similar. But one ingredient, answered prayer, is missing. Why should God answer the prayer of someone who disregards a part of His being, namely, His Son? My human reaction is to be offended when someone slights one of my children. And perhaps the slight is deserved. God's Son is perfect. It is fair that God require that we accept Him. So our first qualification for answered prayer is acceptance of God's Son, Jesus.

Obedience

A second qualification is that our request agrees with the Bible. My husband and I were in the mountains of New York one summer. We had just heard about a bargain trip to Japan. I wanted to go on that trip. I got on my knees and mouthed my desire to God until I was convinced it was His will! No matter that we had no money and a child who would hardly fit in to the travel plans! When my husband told me it was financially impossible I was crushed. Later I discovered 1 Peter 3:1 (LB) "Wives fit in with your husband's plans." Had I known of that verse earlier, it would have saved prayertime that could have been better used.

Get Acquainted with God

Spending time absorbing the Bible is essential for answered prayer. It is unfair for us to ask Him to get us out of trouble, make our days unruffled, and solve our problems when we haven't been trying to get better acquainted with Him. As we get to know Him better, we're more aware of what we should be. We know more of God's nature; and we know more of the nature He wants us to have.

In reading the Old Testament, we learn that God answered prayer in proportion to the obedience of His people. "Offer unto God thanksgiving; and pay the vows unto the Most High. And call upon Me in the day of trouble; I will deliver thee, and thou shalt glorify Me" (Ps. 50:14-15, KJV).

We live in an age of grace; however, obedience is still important. "Now we know that God heareth not sinners; but if any man be a worshipper of God, *and doeth His will,* him He heareth" (John 9:31 KJV).

Reading the Bible is one step to answered prayer, but not the only step. "Be ye doers of the Word and not hearers only" (James 1:22, KJV). Knowing the Bible, certificates from seminars, and complete sets of tapes on scriptural principles do not make us obedient.

Bend Your Will

I was holding onto a pet sin tenaciously. I had excuses, but they were crutches to support my own selfishness. I didn't *want* to give up my "pet." No wonder I was hobbling along spiritually. It's hard to stop rationalizing and obey. But why should God listen to me when I don't listen to Him? Why should He move His hands in response to my prayers when I won't move mine in obedience to His request?

"And whatsoever we ask, we receive of Him, because we keep His commandments, and do those things that are pleasing in His sight" (1 John 3:22, KJV).

Obey is not a popular word in our world today. People disregard authority at all levels. Cynicism is our first reaction to directions we're given. We wonder, "How can I get around that?" This is not God's way. He wants our steel wills to bend to Him. He provides us with lots of exercises in bending: government directives, employer-employee relationships, and relationships within the body of believers, to name a few. We profit from obedience in those relationships. But the greater gain is that we *learn to obey*. We transfer the ability to bend to our relationship to God. That is His intention. Examine your actions and attitude in the light of Scripture. Maybe you have some obeying to do.

God Is Sovereign

A word of caution is necessary here. Unanswered prayer is not *always* due to disobedience. It *may be* sometimes. We can become judgmental if we see unanswered prayer in the lives of our friends and appoint ourselves a committee-of-one to find the sin that caused it. One woman suffered mental and emotional agony for months because God did not seem to be answering a specific prayer. She was searching her life to see where she needed to change. Her objective: she wanted a Yes answer from God. She could find no apparent area where she was disobedient to Him. Looking back on those months now, my friend sees that God was giving her a faith-expanding test. Would she trust Him even when He seemed to be silent? What a precious lesson to learn.

Faith

God loves to answer prayers that are asked in faith. We are told in Hebrews 11:6 that it is impossible to please God without faith. He wants us to come to Him believing He is big enough and powerful enough to do anything. He wants us to believe that He is, and that He is the "rewarder of those who diligently seek Him" (Heb. 11:6, KJV).

Does faith seem like some abstract characteristic that is beyond your grasp? There is a popular notion today that it doesn't matter what the object of your faith is—just so you have faith. This notion, though popular, is wrong. That idea reminds me of a balloon: lots of nothing with a positive mental attitude stretched over it. It floats along looking pretty till the pressure is on. It would be like saying a person can sit anywhere if he *believes* a chair is under him. No matter how much he believes a chair is beneath him, he will end up on the floor if his faith is not based on fact.

It is logical for us to place our faith in God. We are told of His personhood in Scripture and know Him to be worthy of our faith. He is the Creator of everything, including each of us as unique beings. He has complete knowledge of us and every other person or circumstance in our lives. There is no limit to His power. He is stable. The characteristics and power that He possessed thousands of years ago are exactly the same today. But the characteristic that makes Him most worthy of our faith is that He loves us. He wants only our good. "No good thing does He withhold from those who walk uprightly" (Ps. 84:11).

Faith Building

Here are a few faith-building exercises. Study God. Discover all you can about Him—what He has done and what He wants to do. You will discover that He deserves your faith. Secondly, consider His supreme act of love toward you: turning His back on His only Son so that He could enjoy fellowship with you. As you study these areas, and let your mind consider His being, your faith and love for Him cannot help but grow. Thirdly, let Him prove Himself worthy of your faith. We often live doing only what we can safely handle in our own strength. This doesn't require much faith. Has He laid something in front of you that seems like an impossibility, considering your abilities and energy (as you see them)? Praise the Lord and launch out. Let God show you the Nancy, or Sarah, or Karen that He sees!

These exercises will help you put into practice Hebrews 4:16: "Let us therefore come boldly unto the throne of grace, that we may obtain mercy, and find grace to help in time of need" (KJV).

Confidence

As your faith grows and you become more intimate in your relationship with God, you can exercise confidence in His presence. This boldness is not arrogance or pride; it is simply living confidence. You are in the presence of One who loves you more than any human could. You are not pleading for attention from an aloof, distracted, supercomputer. You are communicating with your intimate Friend. He wants you there. Expect Him to do "exceedingly abundantly above all that we ask or think" (Eph. 3:20, KJV).

Forgiveness

God wants us to pray with a clear conscience. We cannot do this if there is conflict and bitterness in our relationships. We must be open and free of guilt in our relationship with Him, and also with other people. "And whenever you stand praying, forgive, if you have anything against anyone; so that your Father also who is in heaven may forgive you your transgressions" (Mark 11:25). Second Corinthians 2:7 tells us one reason why God wants us to forgive: ". . . you should rather forgive and comfort him, lest somehow such a one be overwhelmed by excessive sorrow."

When we have been offended, we may not know why. Many times the person who hurt us is carrying a burden and having a hard time coping. Rather than an unforgiving and cold spirit, that person needs our comfort. Forgiving changes the way we smile at that person. Forgiving restores a spirit of calm to our mind, heart, and body. It opens the way for the relationship to be healed.

In the Book of Matthew, we learn that God did not want an offering from a person involved in a fractured relationship. "Therefore if thou bring thy gift to the altar, and there rememberest that thy brother hath ought against thee; leave there thy gift before the altar, and go thy way; first be reconciled to thy brother, and then come and offer thy gift" (Matt. 5:23-24, KJV). God wants us to come to Him in love. He sees how much we love Him by our love for people: ". . . for he that loveth not his brother whom he hath seen, how can he love God whom he hath not seen? And this commandment have we from Him, that he who loveth God love his brother also" (1 John 4:20-21, KJV).

Forgiveness is a requirement for love. We are not perfect. No matter how wonderful our relationship with husband, mother, father, or friend, there are times when we need to forgive or be forgiven. What freshness and vigor it gives to the relationship!

While I was confessing my sins and asking for forgiveness one day, a cousin came to mind. In high school we had been competitors but not friends. We were both Christians but no one would have guessed it by the feelings shown between us. We had vied for honors and positions. God *could* have been glorified had we excelled together and loved each other. (Our parents would have been happier too!) There had been little contact since high school days, but I knew what God wanted me to do.

I sat down and wrote a long letter. It was hard to ask for forgiveness; it was harder to admit why I needed forgiveness. Several pages and many tears later, what freshness and joy I felt! God's healing did not stop there. I received a volume of computer pages in return onto which my cousin poured out her heart. We can now praise the Lord together for what He has taught us. The testimony of our high school years cannot be changed. But we are being changed, and our families will be.

How Do I Pray?

The ability to pray does not come automatically when we become Christians. Our Lord's disciples asked Him to teach them to pray (Luke 11:1). We can ask Him to teach us also. It's helpful to study the prayers in the Bible. We can use them as a basis for our prayers.

I often find that I do not know how to pray for my children. Economics, international affairs, and technology are changing so rapidly that their future may be in a different world from mine. However, I can take Paul's words in Colossians and make them my own. "Dear Lord, help Valerie understand what You want her to do; make her wise about spiritual things. May the way she lives always please You and honor You. Help her to always be doing good, kind things for others, while all the time learning to know You better and better." (My paraphrase of Col. 1:9-10, LB)

Do you want to praise God? Mary's Magnificat (Luke 1:46-55) may help you communicate your worship.

With the wealth of Scripture on prayer, there are still times when we cannot utter a word. Sometimes, we hurt too much to think clearly. Sometimes, we are so overwhelmed with agony that no words can express our feelings. The Holy Spirit follows through when we cannot, and presents our concerns before the Lord. "And in the same way the Spirit also helps our weakness; for we do not know how to pray as we should, but the Spirit Himself intercedes for us with groanings too deep for words" (Rom. 8:26).

We are told in Scripture to "pray constantly" (1 Thes. 5:17, RSV). For most of us, that means we must pray "on the hoof." Few women can take large chunks of time during the day and find a quiet corner for prayer. However, I find that in order to be prayer-oriented all day, I must have some quiet prayertime before the day's activities begin. This is not God's requirement, but it makes His "pray constantly" instruction functional for me. During this time I concentrate on what God is and I praise Him for His character. I thank Jesus for what He has done so that I can pray. I show God my calendar for the day and ask Him to sort out what He doesn't want there. I give him the hours of the day. Many times He adds things. Within this framework it's so much easier to communicate during the day over vacuum or laundry or study desk, flat tire, or whatever.

Sometimes, our family writes down what we've laid out before the Lord. Then we record when and how He answers. During April of 1973, I prayed earnestly for a child. Almost a year went by and it appeared that God's answer was No or Wait. I was wrong. He was answering my prayer but not in the way I had expected. In April of 1974, God added to our family, by adoption, a beautiful 2-month-old son. He had been conceived when I began praying.

Being Is More Than Doing

Some confusion regarding prayer is due to our idea of God's will for our lives. We want to be praying in God's will, but we feel we don't know His will; therefore, we don't how to pray.

Perhaps we are not aware of the fact that God is primarily concerned with our *being* rather than our *doing*. We want to know which job He wants us to take. He wants us to be content and look to Him as the ultimate source for our needs regardless of where we work (likely, He could use us in either job).

We want to know which man we should marry. He can make a beautiful marriage of any two Christians. He is concerned with whether we are willing to let Him teach us to love our mate. Yes, God can do anything with circumstances, but He usually doesn't begin there. He begins with us.

I prayerfully looked for God's direction one spring as to whether I should return to my job in the fall. God's direction was to return. However, one disaster after another happened during that school year in connection with my job. Had I misread God's will? No. I became "too busy" with job, family, and home to begin every day with my Lord. Irritability, lack of direction, and other problems robbed me of peace and my life of the effectiveness there might have been.

In the process of *doing*, I had neglected what God wanted me to *become*. More important than where I spent my time was how I lived each hour. If you're in the place God wants you to be but you lack love, patience, peace, joy and/or any other fruit of the Spirit, you are out of God's will.

King Hezekiah was dying. He was 39 years old and had been King of Judah for 14 years. He pleaded with God to give him more time, and God granted 15 additional years. Hezekiah's life had been marked by spiritual victories. But from this time on, disaster moved in. He proudly showed off "his" material goods to another king. He begat Manasseh who reigned with such corruption that we cringe at reading 2 Kings 21. When the prophet Isaiah told him that his people would be taken captive because of his folly, Hezekiah said in effect "At least there will be peace in my day, so everything's good." His concern: his own personal pleasure. God's permissive will for Hezekiah to live 15 more years became Hezekiah's license to do things his way.

Fasting

A partner of prayer is fasting. During Jesus' time, many people wanted others to know when they were fasting so that they would be regarded as superspiritual. Because this misuse was so common, Jesus gave instructions about fasting to His followers (Matt. 6:16-18). *"Whenever* you fast" means that Jesus expected that His followers would fast—but not while He was on earth. Fasting was for after He had returned to His Father (Matt. 9:15). However, Jesus Himself fasted. (Matt. 4:2).

We find that in the Old Testament, fasting and prayer were practices through which God's people showed Him their desire for direction. "To seek of Him a right way for us" (Ezra 8:21, KJV), David led the people in their fasting. It can be a way by which we show God the sincerity of our hearts. When we fast, we are putting aside our freedom to eat in order to concentrate on our Lord. We see in Acts 13:2 that while the church at Antioch was "ministering to the Lord and fasting," the Holy Spirit gave them direction.

Perhaps it is overlooked today because our society does not emphasize self-discipline. Our culture is pleasure-oriented. Self-gratification is the basis for most activity (or lack of it). Self-discipline is required for fasting.

"All things are lawful for me, but not all things are profitable. All things are lawful for me, but I will not be mastered by anything. Food is for the stomach, and the stomach is for food; but God will do away with both of them. Yet the body is not for immorality, but for the Lord; and the Lord is for the body" (1 Cor. 6:12-13).

Fasting helps you remember that your physical needs are in your Father's hands. Taking care of physical needs can consume a disproportionate amount of time and energy. Fasting reminds you that your bodies are not eternal.

When you feel hungry, accept that as a prayer reminder. Time usually spent in meal preparation and eating can be used in prayer. Fasting is a way to humble yourself.

One side benefit of fasting is that it sharpens your appreciation of food. Few people in the United States ever experience hunger. After fasting, one is more thankful to God for what one usually takes for granted.

How Do I Fast?

If fasting is a new spiritual exercise for you, study Scripture about it, asking God to be your Teacher. When you set aside a time to fast, you might memorize some verses related to prayer to consider during the day.

Sometimes, I choose a special topic of prayer for a day of fasting based on the eight goals for fasting in Isaiah 58:6-7. "Is this not the fast which I chose, *To loosen the bond of wickedness, To undo the bands of the yoke. And to let the oppressed go free,* And *break every yoke? Is it not to divide your bread with the hungry, And bring the homeless poor into the house; When you see the naked, to cover him, And not to hide yourself from your own flesh?*"

To be specific, I pray for the Lord to show us more ways to share what He's given us. I pray that my children will not be bound by sin. And I pray for myself, that sins that reach into my life will be broken.

Fasting seems to unleash God's power in our lives in a fresh way. "Then your light will break out like the dawn, and your recovery will speedily spring forth; and your righteousness will go before you; The glory of the Lord will be your rear guard" (Isa. 58:8).

Is it the act of giving up of food that unleashes God's power? No. It is the fact that we are willing to give up *anything* in order for God to work through us.

Are you waiting anxiously for an answer to prayer? God's desire to answer is greater than yours! "It will also come to pass that before they call, I will answer; and while they are still speaking, I will hear" (Isa. 65:24).

But even more than what He can do for us, He wants us to delight in *Him*. "Delight yourself in the Lord; and He will give you the desires of your heart. Commit your way to the Lord, trust also in Him, and He will do it" (Ps. 37:4-5).

5.
Blueprint for Oneness

"And now I present to you Mr. and Mrs. Robert Neff." The music was supposed to burst out joyfully after those words. Since the church had no musical instruments, a record was to provide the recessional. Nothing happened. There was complete silence. Bob and I started down the aisle anyway. We were halfway to the back of the church when, after scratching and whining, the record got underway. After that beginning we had nowhere to go in our marriage but up.

Most couples believe, like we did, that life after the marriage ceremony will be one joyful symphony. Many are surprised and disappointed to find that the music and bells fall silent.

One friend whose marriage lasted less than a year described his experience, "All of my worst dreams of marriage came true." Some persistent couples hang together and build a relationship. Forty percent do not. What makes the difference? An important aspect is how we view marriage.

The 45-minute period preceding our silent exit had been the most important transaction in our lives, aside from our individual commitments to Christ. For 19 years I had built relationships with parents, sisters, other relatives, and friends. There were strong bonds in those ties. But now God saw my bond with Bob as the strongest in my life. I had known him for 16 months. Bob had built family relationships for 23 years. But now his direction from Scripture was to leave them to cleave to me (Gen. 2:24 and Matt. 19:5). Our bond was to be so strong that if we were pulled in opposite directions, we would sooner lose an arm or a part of ourselves than let go of each other.

If we cement two logs together and then try to pull them apart, the logs will split before the cement bond breaks. That kind of "cleaving" is rare in marriages today. But that's the kind of union that marriage was intended to be.

True Love?

Two people meet. They can't believe all they have in common. Their favorite late night snack is olive burgers. They both like to water ski. They enjoy the same kind of music, and there is a special excitement they sense when in the same room together. It doesn't occur to them that they might have similar feelings for one fourth of the members of the opposite sex.

Surely marriage was meant to follow. They are guessing that their feelings of closeness will grow. They are gambling that their common preferences will give them more pleasure than the pain of similar problems.

They have never thought to discuss their ideas on children or consider what they'd like to be doing in 25 years. They have not carefully examined the parents of their potential mate. It is often said you don't marry your in-laws. That's true. You don't have to. Their main personality traits, values, and ideas are built into your mate. You will live with them long after your in-laws are gone.

As with all gambling, the odds are uneven. There is a chance that this couple will negotiate a successful marriage. The odds are greater that they won't.

It isn't long before alienation sets in. It may be followed by a legal divorce. Or it may become a well-hidden separation, an emotional divorce. In any case, there is no oneness. If there is an emotional divorce, most outsiders are unaware of the grand canyon in the marriage between husband and wife. In fact, the couple may be to that point where the chasm is growing wider without their awareness. Perhaps one knew but didn't speak up. The result is the same. There is no cleaving, no interdependence, *no oneness*.

Programmed for Failure

Sometimes, it seems that a marriage is programmed for failure before it begins. Why? Many people approach marriage with the idea that their relationship can exist as long as they "feel" good together. Marriage often takes place when the young people are going through a temporary swing away from their youthful life-style. They are caught up with numbers: My peers are doing it. This is a disastrous reason to marry. The person who comes along at this time (even though he is the wrong person) is IT.

The couple may have discussed marriage at length—with others who are unmarried, or with newlyweds who have no track record. They avoid the old fogies, grandparents, and other has-beens.

It is very likely that one or both members of the couple have not yet recognized their worth as persons—or the inherent worth of their prospective mate. It is also likely that they have not developed communication skills and are not consciously making room for each other to be whole persons in their relationship.

First Criterion

The first criterion for Christian marriage is that both be committed to Christ. God was the Originator of marriage. The institution was designed to function in conjunction with a total life commitment to Him. "Be ye not bound together with unbelievers: for what partnership have righteousness and lawlessness, or what fellowship has light with darkness?" (2 Cor. 6:14)

When a Christian marries a non-Christian, there is a built-in chasm which will never close, unless the nonbeliever commits himself to Christ. The chasm usually becomes wider. Their minds have two different orientations. "But a natural man does not accept the things of the Spirit of God; for they are foolishness to him, and he cannot understand them, because they are spiritually appraised. But he who is spiritual appraises all things, yet he himself is appraised by no man" (1 Cor. 2:14–15).

A non-Christian mate will not understand your desire to give money to an institution for which he feels no empathy. He will not understand the closeness you feel to a Christian though you have just met. He will not understand why you are lonely. It is apparent to him that the two of you are together. It is not apparent to him that your spirit wants to be with a group of believers, and that lacking the intimacy of fellowship with other believers, there is a void that he cannot fill.

The God who loves you wants the best for you. "No good thing does He withhold from those who walk uprightly" (Ps. 84:11). His guideline is that you select a Christian mate. Having done that, however, there is no guarantee of a "happily ever after." Next, we must choose God's blueprint for marriage.

What Is Love?

The most basic ingredient in God's blueprint for marriage is love. It sounds so simple. Most couples would say "Of course we love each other." The question could be asked, "If loving your husband were a crime, could you produce evidence enough to be convicted?" If feelings could not be introduced as evidence and you were not permitted to take the stand, how would your case be proven?

"We've been living under the same roof for 15 years." Or, "There's Chris who's 10, Larry who's 8, Mary is 6, and Judy is 5."

But what is love? How do we live it?

Love is not so ambiguous when we study Scripture. We see that it is learned. Titus 2 tells us that older women are to teach younger women to love their husbands. We know that it is an act of the will. We are *told* to love our neighbor as we love ourselves. If we can be instructed to love it must be that we can determine with our wills to obey that instruction and love. Love changes our behavior. First Corinthians 13 tells what behavioral characteristics a person possesses who loves. The love is *agape* love, the same love that God has for us. And here Paul is telling us it is the same kind of love we should have for each other. The characteristics of love are not compatible with immaturity.

Behavioral Characteristics of Love:	Evidence of Lack of Love:
is slow to lose patience	is possessive
looks for ways of being constructive	is anxious to impress
has good manners	inflates its own importance
shares joy	pursues selfish advantage
is unlimited in endurance	is touchy (takes offense)
is completely trusting (loyal)	keeps account of evil
is always hopeful	gloats over another person's error
outlasts anything	

That love is an act of the will explains why arranged marriages can be successful. Two strangers, selected for each other by parents, learn to love each other. They commit their wills to loving.

This also explains why couples after many years of apparent love can decide they don't belong together anymore. We can decide to stop loving. We can stop learning to love. We can will not to love. We can, through unintentional neglect, allow other emotional involvements to crowd out love for our mate. We will only begin to learn what love is on this earth. But we can begin!

Love Is Expensive
The scriptural love that is required in marriage

costs. It costs to be "always hopeful" when your husband has lost the seventh job in 12 years. You must win an emotional battle within yourself to believe that he will find another job. It may be a physical battle to get out of bed and prepare his breakfast before he leaves to go job hunting.

It costs to endure unearned criticism day after day and at the same time look for ways to praise him so he will no longer need to criticize. No wonder love has to be learned. It could never come naturally to us in our original selfish state.

This love in Scripture desires but does not demand anything in return. What a contrast to common love today! "Love can and should stop when the object of his or her affections rejects that love in favor of someone else. Love is too valuable to be wasted on someone who doesn't want it" (Lena Levine and David Loth, *The Emotional Sex: Why Women Are the Way They Are Today*. New York: William Morrow). What if Jesus had lived by those words? God the Father would never have allowed His Son to come to earth on those conditions. Man had been rejecting God since his creation. But God loved anyway. Jesus gave anyway. The example of love for us is clear. My love for my husband does not depend on him. It depends on me.

Conditioned Love

We have allowed ourselves to be conformed to this world. We have conformed to *eros* love as a basis for marriage. This love is based on physical desire. It is human passion to satisfy ourselves. Love of an adorable object is our present day definition. If the person is adorable, love him. If he is worthy, love him; for better or best or not at all.

We have conformed to a Skinnerian view of ourselves. B.F. Skinner is a behavioral psychologist who has proposed that behavior can be determined by external rewards. According to Skinner, our responses are determined by external stimuli. (This assumes we are blank originally and develop solely on the basis of stimulus-response sequences in our lives.) When we accept or internalize this theory, then our love is dependent on what stimulates us, or fails to stimulate. Our love becomes conditioned by external circumstances, not God-directed obedience.

An example of this is the "I can't help myself" syndrome. As Christians, we have internalized this fallacy. We are saying, "I am nothing inside; I can only respond to what confronts me. I have no control over my environment or my reactions." We "fall" in love.

We may walk, run, or fly with God but He never initiates our falling! He does *not* initiate irresponsible behavior on our part. One girl told me about the person she was going to marry. She said she had fallen in love and couldn't help herself. She went on describing the marvelous characteristics of her intended. I knew she was a Christian and he was not. She had internalized that sometimes she just *had* to act and feel certain ways, without engaging her mind first.

This type of mind-set explains why Hitler could lead his people, why "nobody's in charge here," why there are bumper stickers that say, "Act now, think later."

This mind-set denies that we are created as intelligent beings in God's image. God must want to turn His head when He sees humans behave as nonhuman robots.

Learn to Love

How is love learned? It is learned best by example. Hopefully, husband and wife will have learned how to love in a Christian home from Christian parents. But that is not always the case. With the increase of divorce in our Christian community it will occur less frequently. If you have married a man who does not know how to love, he can learn from your example.

If a person can't cook we don't lock him out of the kitchen till he learns. We accept his less than desirable burnt offerings and praise any appearance of success. We demonstrate, we encourage. Learning love is similar. The most effective, efficient way to learn is by example. We continually remind ourselves to put the other person's best interests first and live love ourselves. It is our human reaction to say, "He's not looking out for my best interests, so I'll have to." But what example of love will he have to imitate then, Scripture tells us how love acts. We will to act in that pattern in obedience to God. This is love.

Submission

Another ingredient in God's blueprint for marriage is submission. This is not a word for women only. It is a word for the whole world.

I have watched with interest Margaret Mead's observations of cultures. For 50 years this noted anthropologist has studied women, men, cultures, and the world as an interdependent community. She recently described the world community as "a miscellaneous cafeteria of disasters, a shopping list for nowhere." She admitted, "I'm painting a discouraging picture. . . . In the '60s, kids thought there was an establishment. If they could just get at it, they could fix it. Now they realize that nobody is in charge" (Lecture at Northwestern University, Evanston, Illinois, November 10, 1977). The results of this void in leadership have been misuse of our environmental resources, wealth, comfort, and ease for some humans; starvation for others. Margaret Mead's solution is this: to "invoke in every individual a sense of responsibility for the world." She believes we must acknowledge that we are our brother's keeper. This requires submission, putting aside our personal desires for the benefit of others and the good of the whole, ourselves included.

Webster defines *submission* as the "surrender of person and power to the control of another." Though the world has not acknowledged this need of humankind, God did. Having created us, He knew our composition and need. Where there is interdependence, there must be order. Governments fail when order is lacking. Business flops and traffic jams. Marriage partners wrestle to a stalemate. Submission is the oil required for a beautifully interdependent relationship.

We submit to each other by looking out for our mate's best interests. "And be subject to one another in the fear of Christ" (Eph. 5:21). We do not have to wonder what God's specific direction is to us. "Wives, be subject to your own husbands, as to the Lord. For the husband is the head of the wife, as Christ also is the head of the church, He Himself being the Saviour of the body. But as the church is subject to Christ, so also the wives ought to be to their husbands in everything" (Eph. 5:22-25).

How can we be submissive to our less than perfect mates? We can adapt to them (or fit in with their plans) as to the Lord. We recognize that it is our Lord's instruction to us so we adapt to our husbands for Christ's sake.

Wives are told to submit *themselves*. No husband can *make* his wife be submissive. He can make her go through the motions of obeying him, but that is not submission. Only the individual can determine, by an act of her will, to put aside herself as her primary concern and put her husband first.

When are we to be submissive? In what set of circumstances? Above or under what conditions? Verse 25 tells us "in everything." This is logical. Can you imagine the power struggle if we were told that we were to be submissive in some areas and not others? There would be endless arguments. Does this issue fit under the "together" column or the "do your own thing column"?

Marriage is two people committing every area of their lives to each other. There is no private corner that we can keep separate. We cannot have a pet area where we make decisions without considering the effect on our mate.

Why are we to be submissive? Because God placed our husband in the position as head in the marriage relationship. The fact that God did it should be a sufficient basis for us to accept it. If we desire to search for reasons why, we find many in Scripture. First Corinthians 11:9 tells us that woman was created for man, not vice versa. Genesis 2:18 tells us that woman was created to be "a helper suitable for him." First Peter 3:7 suggests that woman is the weaker vessel. As women we should not be threatened by the realization that God had different intentions in creating man and woman. Throughout Scripture we see that God is glorified by diversity. Romans 12 tells us that it is God's intention that there be diversity in the body of believers. A study of the personalities of the apostles is a study in individuality.

We look to the created world and see diversity. Each person has a unique fingerprint. Cells within the body are highly differentiated. I have never seen two trees that cast the same shadow or heard two waves roll in with the same roar. This diversity nourishes us. Watching waves is therapeutic; not because they march to shore like robots, but because no two are alike.

In much greater ways, we are nourished by the diversity of male and female. Submission oils that interdependent relationship.

Align Yourself

I looked up the idea of submission in *Vines Expository Dictionary* and read that the word was "primarily a military term, to rank under" (Vol. 4, Old Tappan, N.J.: Fleming H. Revell). While there are other meanings for the word, I personally like to think of submission in this way. A soldier aligns himself with the one in command because they are both putting all their efforts into one objective. One cannot function effectively without the other. There is no loss for one without loss to the other. Conversely, one cannot win alone. Victory for one is victory for both.

There is an important principle underlying the concept of women aligning themselves with their husbands. Alignment is for a purpose, a common goal which motivates the relationship.

At this point, we see the potential for marriage

success or failure. God created marriage as a relationship which requires commitment of both man and woman to goals. He knew that they needed this. Before a couple marries, they should determine the goals for their marriage, and more basic, find out what are God's goals for marriage. Throughout their marriage, these purposes need to be rethought, restudied, and then new commitments made to one another and to the goals of the marriage. This will provide added motivation for the husband and wife to cleave to each other.

Many couples today would list mostly economic objectives for their marriage, some of them independent of the relationship, and purely selfish. This programs failure into the home. When selfish goals are not obtained and there are not higher goals, the couple may have nothing to hold them together. There is no basis for cleaving, and the marriage fails. God's goals for marriage require being together for a lifetime. At no time will a couple be able to check off each item of the list and say, "We're finished; now we can split." I would like to suggest a few goals for Christian marriage:

1. Development of a Christlike character within each partner
2. Development of a relationship which mirrors the relationship of Christ and the church
3. Exercising dominion over the earth
4. Subduing the earth
5. Raising children and instilling into them Christlike character
6. Involvement in a local body which worships the triune God

When we study God's goals and purposes for marriage, we have an important side benefit—a yardstick for measuring priorities. We can look at activities and involvements and ask, "Does this help me align myself with my husband so that we may reach God's goals together?"

Children

God's blueprint for marriage usually includes children. In the love relationship of marriage we are fed emotionally so that we desire to give more. Genesis 1:28 tells us that one of God's *blessings* to man and woman was that they multiply. Children that result from the marriage union are the object of our giving. However, the giving is not one way. Children are part of the maturation process for adults. What parent cannot remember countless times where needs of children *demanded* that parental giving increase beyond what was thought humanly possible. The child has, in a sense, given to his parents the opportunity for maturation. God provides lessons in self-giving through children.

We have long lived in a world marred by sin. One result is that physical problems sometimes prevent a couple from having children. This does not mean that God has denied them children as a source of blessing. It means we are living in a blemished world where all will never be perfect till Christ reigns again. Meanwhile, God can richly bless that childless couple with more of Himself. He may choose to involve them in work that a couple with the demands of children would find hard to handle. That childless couple can delight God's heart. He may place in their family children born to someone else.

However, I wonder if God's heart is saddened by the current trend of couples determining not to have children for selfish reasons. No one will deny that children are an economic drain, to say nothing of the emotional, physical, and intellectual input involved in their upbringing. But God has promised to supply our needs. The supply from Him is never too skimpy to meet the demands. The spiritual stretching that children bring to the marriage relationship will not be laid aside to stagnate in God's economy.

Some couples may feel that bringing another child into this world of crisis is unfair. After taking that issue before the Lord, perhaps such a couple could consider adoption or foster care. Shaping these little people for God is certainly a valid investment.

"Happily ever after" never happens except in storybooks. But who wants to leave out the best part of the love story anyway? It is after the marriage ceremony that Christlikeness is learned. There is a universal purpose for this love story. In the unique relationship of marriage, the world is to see an object lesson of Christ and the church. Does this seem like an unachievable assignment? I hope you answered Yes. Because then you will commit yourself and your marriage to the Lord. And there are no impossible assignments for God.

6.
Beyond Remodeling?

Having studied God's blueprint for marriage you may be saying, "Yes, that sounds good but it's too late for us. The pattern our marriage has taken is beyond remodeling."

It is increasingly popular to say that it's not worth the effort to tear out the old foundation and begin again. Why not call it a failure and begin again with someone else?

That *is* one option. For humanly speaking, there is no such thing as a "fresh start" for a marriage. People are creatures of habit. Every event of our past has some influence on our present being and behavior as it filters through our complex nervous system and brain. Therefore, problems in the past add negative input to the marriage. A couple cannot begin again at zero. They begin to build from a minus figure.

Though divorce and separation are taken lightly in our culture, there is no basis in Scripture for this attitude: "What therefore God has joined together, let no man separate" (Matt. 19:6). Divorce was due to man's heart, not God's. "They said to Him,

'Why then did Moses command to give her a certificate and divorce her?' He said to them, 'Because of your hardness of heart, Moses permitted you to divorce your wives, but from the beginning it has not been this way . . ." (Matt. 19:7-8).

When we see God's general instruction on a matter, our first response should be to obey it. Seldom will that be an impossibility.

Exceptions and Change

When it seems our situation is an exception to God's general instruction, then we need to search Scripture for God's exceptions. He does make them, you know.

In 1 Corinthians 7, Paul told the believers that if a non-Christian mate wished to leave a marriage, the believer should let him go. Also, God permits divorce in the case of unfaithfulness, but does not require it.

Our loving Lord "has called us to peace" (1 Cor. 7:15). It is not His desire that His children live through hell on earth due to seemingly impossible marriage relationships. His usual method for dealing with "impossible" situations, however, is not escape. It is change.

God is a specialist at changing people. Suppose you are in an "impossible" situation. What raw materials does God have to work with? He may not have your mate. He could change external circumstances, but He usually does not begin working there. One source is left. You!

This is true not only in the marriage relationship, but where there is alienation in other relationships, Christian sister with sister, parent with child, employer with employee.

Change Is a Process

Now we must erase one common misconception about change. Usually it is *gradual*, not instant. Yes, God can work with the speed of a comet or in the twinkling of an eye. But He usually does not.

We read of marriages that are transformed by an eight-hour seminar or one chapter of a book. However, most transformations are a *process*. A seed realization takes root. You begin to change your behavior toward your mate. (He may not even notice for a week!) Eventually your change requires a change in him. This may be painful.

Healings for fractured marriages will not be achieved in a day, week, or even a month. The problems have enmeshed over a period of years.

I sometimes talk to a woman who says, "Yes, I tried that, but it didn't work. I put his interests first, for seven years I have . . ." And she explains to me how she has tried to accommodate her husband's behavior. Usually the underlying attitude is, "See what I've put up with?" I feel that she is waiting for me to say, "Yes, it's time now for you to do as you please. He's had more chances than he deserves to shape up." Do we find any basis for this in Scripture? What examples can we find?

The Patience of God

From Genesis to Revelation we see the infinite patience of God. The Old Testament is filled with His continual waiting for His people, the Children of Israel, to turn to Him. He is still waiting for them. The Book of Hosea assures us of God's staying power, though His children turn their backs to Him. He says in Hosea 11:8, "How can I give up? . . . How can I surrender you? . . . My heart is turned over within Me." How could God want His people, in spite of their behavior?

Look at Jesus' example. He came to save the world. What was the response to His love? At first there were crowds of thousands. But He hung on the Cross alone. Did rejection stop Him from loving?

Growth in our spiritual development is not measured by how often God changes circumstances or other people to release us from our dilemmas. In fact, we would stay spiritually immature if only circumstances altered. Yet curiously, stories of outward change are the ones most often shared as evidence of God's working in our lives.

Few people want to share their slow and painful experiences of personal growth and change. We are reluctant to stand up and say, "I was in an impossible dilemma. God has not changed anything in the circumstances but He has changed me and, Praise the Lord, I'm growing!"

Faith Is the Key

When Peter wrote his letters to the church, he mentioned Sarah as an example of a good wife. She could have lived a comfortable life of wealth in a lovely home. But instead, her life was one of continual packing and unpacking, setting up, then moving on. Why? Because of a job promotion or army order? No. Because her husband was "looking for the city which has foundations, whose Architect and Builder is God" (Heb. 11:10).

Abraham put Sarah in some tough spots. Twice she was placed in compromising circumstances because of his lies. Today this would be considered mental cruelty. Yet she stayed with him living in faith, and without fear (1 Peter 3:6; Heb. 11:11).

We have accepted a faulty presupposition regarding marriage: that its permanence is determined by whether our desired results are achieved. Hebrews 11 shows us that visible results are not the primary criteria in God's economy.

We can put a marriage in God's hands in faith just as Abraham put Isaac in God's hands. God required Abraham to be willing for anything to happen to Isaac because he was the Lord's. God did not require Isaac's life. He only required that Abraham be *willing* to release him. We see in Hebrews 11 that many *visible* results of faith occurred. Women's loved ones who had died came to life again. Sarah bore a miracle child. Moses was saved from death as an infant. But beginning with verse 35, though faith is still the key, the visible results are missing.

> . . . and others were tortured, not accepting their release, in order that they might obtain a better resurrection; and other experienced mockings and scourgings, yes, also chains and imprisonment. They were stoned, they were sawn in two, they were tempted, they were put to death with the sword; they went about in sheepskins, in goatskins, being destitute, afflicted, ill-treated (men of whom the world was not worthy), wandering in deserts and mountains and caves and holes in the ground. *And all these, having gained approval through their faith, did not receive what was promised.*

Today, some would probably see these people as spiritual failures. "Since God did not intervene, there must be something wrong in their lives." But Scripture tells us "the world was not worthy" of these people. Their faith enabled them to endure, not to escape.

Moving Toward Maturity

We must be careful in guaranteeing immediate success for all Christian marriages. We are prone to say, "If you do this, you will get this result from your husband." We are programming some people for disappointment. The result: they become bitter toward God. It was their belief that if they came through on X, God would have to respond with Y, and their spouse with Z.

Perhaps God would have liked to, but our mate was unwilling. We must come back to the acknowledgement that we have no guarantee that our mate will change. He may. But he may not ever be what we desire.

Perhaps God has something different for us. We can be sure it will be good because it's from Him. Remember that Jesus' delay in coming to Mary and Martha was in order for them to experience God's best—in that case, their brother being raised from the dead. "And we know that God causes all things to work together for good to those who love God . . ." (Rom. 8:28). God is able to take any person or persons with any kind of past and produce something *good*.

Perhaps God wants to teach someone else a lesson through us. "And all these, having gained approval through their faith, did not receive what was promised, because God had provided something better for us, so that apart from us they should not be made perfect" (Heb. 11:39-40).

These giants of faith had gained God's approval. But God had a bigger job in mind for them. They were to be examples to us. We receive spiritual incentive when we see their dedication and willingness to give up everything for our Lord. They become a part of our personal spiritual maturing.

We see from this that visible results are not the criteria for determining whether marriage is to be permanent.

God Does Not Will Evil

At this point you may be saying, "Must the marriage be preserved then at all costs?" We can agree that divorce is not God's intention. Disease is not God's intention either, nor is death, or devastating floods, or earthquakes. However, they exist in our world and we cannot ignore them.

Alienation is common in many relationships—brother with sister, between people who work together and worship together. God's intention is for forgiveness, love, and growing beyond the alienation.

Today, we are very aware of instances of unfaithfulness in marriage. Some of these are one-time failings, after which forgiveness is sought. One would hope that the other spouse could forgive and go on, though some cannot. There are also sad situations where sins against the marriage go on year after year, with hardly a thought to the harm one is doing in breaking or preventing a marriage. God does make room for exceptions. Though He usually works through our marriage to shape us into Christlikeness, there may be cases in which a mate may be left because of his/her belief in God. We are told to "seek for His kingdom" (Luke 12:31).

As important as marriage is, our personal relationship to Christ comes first. We are assured that whatever we lose for the sake of Jesus, we will receive "many times as much, and shall inherit eternal life" (Matt. 19:29).

Won Without a Word

Recently, a woman told me she wished her unbelieving husband would leave, but he didn't. The Lord began to show her that she would be His instrument in teaching her husband about Christ. Difficult? Yes. His set of values allowed him to live any way he wanted to. She could not. Where Scripture forbade certain behavior, as does Galatians 5:19-21, she had to lovingly tell him she could not do what he was doing. Had she followed him in his behavior she could not claim 1 Peter 3:1-2: "In the same way, you wives, be submissive to your own husbands so that even if any of them are disobedient to the Word, they may be won without a word by the behavior of the wives as they observe your chaste and respectful behavior."

Her behavior had to be chaste (pure and modest) and respectful. Her life might have been easier had God allowed her husband to leave her. But it would not have been as rewarding or fruitful.

Divorce Does Happen

Though we may hurt for our brothers and sisters and friends, and earnestly desire that they not experience the devastation of divorce, it may happen. What should our attitude be toward them then? One of overwhelming love. We are not told in Scripture to ostracize the divorced. We *are* told not even to eat with a lazy man who won't work. The Corinthians were told not to associate with the man who had his father's wife. These are valid reasons to ostracize a fellow Christian. However, we must not lock out our Christian brother or sister because of divorce.

Studies illustrated by a life graph show divorce as the lowest point. (A life graph shows the relative highs and lows in a person's sense of well-being by placing events in graph form.) A person has a greater sense of loss and aloneness in divorce than at the death of a parent. This is intensified by a sense of failure. Many times these emotional upheavals are compounded by the necessity of looking for new housing and by financial pressures and uncertainties. If there are children, they need more emotional reassurance than usual. They ask themselves if they caused daddy or mommy to leave. They may see themselves as less than loveable.

The body of believers can make the difference in whether the divorced will be bitter, trying to live independently from God, or open to spiritual growth.

God Can Provide

In our present court system, the divorce process breeds more hostility between husband and wife. Wounds that result need healing love.

Is there an alternative to this destructive method of divorce? "If then you have law courts dealing with matters of this life, do you appoint them as judges who are of no account in the church? I say this to your shame. Is it so, that there is not among you one wise man who will be able to decide between his brothers, but brother goes to law with brother [or sister], and that before unbelievers? Actually, then, it is already a defeat for you, that you have lawsuits with one another. Why not rather be wronged? Why not rather be defrauded?" (1 Cor. 6:4-7)

Based on this passage the Christian should accept unfair treatment rather than sue another person in court. Does it seem impossible or impractical not to fight for your rights? Humanly speaking, Yes. But God asks us to live above our humanness. Do you feel you must fight for a fair settlement so you won't starve? "And my God shall supply all your needs according to His riches in glory in Christ Jesus" (Phil. 4:19). The provisions of the Lord are more dependable than a court settlement.

Should you be summoned to court, do you feel you would not be adequately represented without a lawyer? How adequate is God! Remember Paul's words, "But the Lord stood with me, and strengthened me" (2 Tim. 4:17).

Take courage from David's psalm: "But let all who take refuge in Thee be glad, let them ever sing for joy; and mayest Thou shelter them, that those who love Thy name may exult in Thee" (Ps. 5:11).

It may sound like the "path of least resistance" to follow God's instruction in 1 Corinthians 6; but it is not an easy path to follow today. Pressure from everywhere shouts, "But no one does it that way!" It takes spiritual strength to place ourselves, our rights, and our children in God's hands. He may be our only Source of reassurance.

Learn to Know God

Consider Job. His friends had enough advice for him to bring on a case of depression. They argued from the viewpoint of tradition: experience from the past shows this. We must keep going to God's Word to make sure we are where *He* wants us to be. This gives us courage. Then we can say with Job, "I know that Thou canst do all things, and that no purpose of Thine can be thwarted. 'Who is this that hides counsel without knowledge?' Therefore, I have declared that which I did not understand. Things too wonderful for me, which I did not know" (Job 42:2-3).

When Job answered his friends, he spoke based on what he knew of God. It seemed the visible evidence was on their side. But what is the conclusion? "I have heard of Thee by the hearing of the ear; but now my eye sees Thee" (Job 42:5).

When Job acted, based on what he knew of God, God rewarded his faith by letting him see results. All that Job had "given up for God" was not only restored, but multiplied. God's promise of Luke 12:31 was in effect then. "But seek for His kingdom; and these things shall be added to you."

Doesn't the Church Care?

It is not my intention to undermine confidence in lawyers or imply that the court system can never be used by Christians. But it is my observation that we have placed our future and our confidence in them, rather than God. And in some ways this is understandable. Through my close experience with friends who have had legal difficulties due to divorce, I have, with sadness, seen the reluctance or inadequacy of their churches to become involved to any significant and decisive extent.

Because of what I saw, I contacted seven prominent evangelical churches in the United States, to ask them what they would do if someone with legal problems came to them for counsel and decision. The staff members I talked with seemed baffled by the question. Some said they would try to resolve the situation by pastoral counseling.

We seem to be in a dilemma in which many churches are not taking a biblical position in this matter. Their members either assume that they have no recourse but the courts, or run up against the inability or unwillingness of the church leaders to act.

God, the Creator of marriage, gives us guidelines to make marriage joyful and fulfilling. If our marriage is not that, we do not take it from our Creator's hands, give it to an "objective third party" to repair or destroy. We place it in His hands:
"Do not fear, for I am with you; Do not anxiously look about you, for I am your God. I will strengthen you, Surely I will help you. Surely I will uphold you with My righteous right hand" (Isa. 41:10).

7.
Marriage and Master Charge

Several years ago, my husband went to Washington, D.C. on business. His departure was like so many others—I dropped him off at O'Hare. His plane was a little late. Everything was "business as usual" for the Neffs. His arrival four days later was different.

During his absence I had discovered a sale on carpets. Unfortunately, none of the "sale" carpets suited my taste, but they happened to have another that I couldn't pass up. I had originally entered the store thinking I would buy carpeting for one bedroom. With such a fantastic sale, the cost would be reasonable. While I shopped and browsed, I wondered if at this price, I should "save" more and carpet two bedrooms.

With my mind in gear to carpet two rooms, I now moved to a more expensive carpet. The store didn't have what I wanted for the second room. But no matter, I ordered one and went to a nearby department store to see their merchandise. They didn't have any carpeting that appealed to me, but fortunately, I had entered the store during a "Grand Opening" sale. (Why "Grand Opening" I don't know. The store had been there for years.) The first few items I purchased, I had to rationalize a bit to justify buying. With inflation, wouldn't it make sense to buy a copper chafing dish now rather than in five years? (I tripped over the monstrosity on legs in my attic this week. All seven pieces clattered, reminding me I had used it three times.)

Before long, I was joyfully saving money in many departments without even needing to rationalize. Unfortunately I ran out of shopping time. But that didn't matter. The following day, my teacher friend and I zipped out on our lunch hour. Being Armenian, she knew just where to buy carpeting. We were successful.

The day Bob was to return, I had a minor mishap with our Volkswagen. I crashed into the brick base of our school sign. The students found this funny and I laughed too. After all, the car was still drivable.

The trip back from the airport was not so funny. As I bubbled on about my fantastic savings, my exhausted husband became quieter by the sentence. His mind was not adding up the "saved" column but the "spent" column. It did not amuse him that the one functioning car headlight focused down into the curb rather than on the expressway. If emotional temperature could affect a car, we should have parked a car dripping with icicles in our driveway. Miriam had saved nearly a hundred dollars. Bob's wife had spent nearly a thousand. It was enough to make a man fear leaving town!

Marriage and Money

Money had become one of the biggest sources of

conflict in our marriage. In my case, it was more than a marriage-and-money problem. It was a spiritual problem. Acquiring things became an objective to look forward to. "I'll do this next in this room." "I can't wait till I can replace that." I was actually saying, "I'll be happier when I have ———." This is sin. "Not that I speak from want; for I have learned to be content in whatever circumstances I am" (Phil. 4:11).

Real contentment is in knowing how to be happy with the Lord and with what He provides. I wish I had learned this lesson earlier. For most people, the acquiring of money is not an end in itself. It is what money brings them which becomes the objective.

Money Meanings

In our society, money means things and status. To some extent it means security. The world's view of money is aptly expressed in Ecclesiastes. "Money is a protection" (7:12) and "money is the answer to everything" (10:19).

The objectives of status and security are not wrong in themselves. But as a Christian, my source for meeting these objectives is my Lord, not money. He has promised to supply all my needs (Phil. 4:19). My status comes from Him. Knowing I am His creation and the special object of His love gives me inner contentment that is beyond the temporary lift of a new outfit, car, or plush environment. My security is in Him.

How do we become so entangled with financial problems? The answer is extremely simple. We become conformed to this world. We allow ourselves to adapt to the materialism in which we live.

Our minds function as if we were not God's children: as if *we* were in charge, not God. The result: selfishness. We grasp for all we can. "For the love of money is a root of all sorts of evil, and some by longing for it have wandered away from the faith, and pierced themselves with many a pang" (1 Tim. 6:10).

In my case, money problems in my marriage were the visible tip of the iceberg of selfishness. Of course, I should have all these things. I was a pretty good wife; I was willing to work. If I didn't spend the money, who would? I. I. I. God had allowed us to have the tool of money. I had handed it over to Satan. He was using it to chisel our marriage apart.

Freedom?

As a Christian, I was the possessor of a unique characteristic: freedom. "For you were called to freedom . . ." (Gal. 5:13). That was my spiritual position. But my everyday behavior didn't match my position.

I did *not feel free* arguing with my husband over money. I did *not feel free* trying to explain purchases that were unnecessary. I was *not free* to budget. There was no money left to manage after paying the bills. I was *not free* to decide on spending priorities. The paycheck already committed.

Sound familiar? If you are in a similar situation, your mind spends many hours wrestling with financial conflicts rather than working toward more important objectives. This worry then drains your emotional energy.

Paul's admonition to Timothy to avoid the love of money is capped with these statement. "But flee from these things, you man of God; and pursue righteousness, godliness, faith, love, perseverance and gentleness. Fight the good fight of faith; take hold of the eternal life to which you were called, and you made the good confession in the presence of many witnesses" (1 Tim. 6:11-12). Satan knows that we cannot give attention to these objectives if we are bound by financial conflict.

Solutions

What is the solution to the money dilemma? There are two concepts that have freed our family from financial pressure. (1) Recognizing that God is in charge of the purse strings. It's His money and through Him we must be effective stewards using this valuable tool. (2) Making a family financial plan and living according to that plan. Let's look at these two areas in greater detail.

1. *Recognizing that God is in charge of the purse strings.* God "richly supplies us with all things to enjoy" (1 Tim. 6:17).

Everything that we have, money or things, comes from God. He enables us to earn paychecks. If we are given things, these belong to Him because we are His. Acknowledging this fact means we will be good stewards of money and things. "He who did not spare His own Son, but delivered Him up for us all, how will He not also with Him freely give us all things?" (Rom. 8:32)

I looked out my kitchen window one rainy fall morning. Raindrops splattered on our shiny new charcoal grill which I had neglected to bring in the night before. Stewardship. I dashed out and pulled it into the garage. This incident may seem insignificant; however, it was the beginning of a new thought pattern for me. Each thing "I" own is the Lord's. The more mileage we get from it through wise use and care, the more profitable stewards we are. Our grill could rust in one season. Or it could be used for years and free money to be put to other purposes for the Lord. Acknowledging that our living room and its furniture is the Lord's means that it will be used and not sit idle while everyone marches to the basement.

I marvel at how the Lord has provided our things. Our beautiful baby grand piano was practically free. (The moving charge was almost as much as the purchasing charge.) Yes, it required stripping and refinishing. We purchased two new chairs without legs for next to nothing. This provided Bob with a brain-teaser. He enjoyed finding legs for those chairs much more than wrestling with the checkbook after I'd been on a spending spree. It seems that the Lord has provided what we need for much less than we expected since we have given Him the purse strings.

An important result of being God's financial stewards is that we can win the psychological battle to spend. When I see a sign that says SAVE NOW, I don't fly into spending gear. My day will not be ruined if I have not "saved" 20 percent. In fact, I will experience more satisfaction at the end of the day if I have saved 100 percent by not buying.

When I see advertising that tries to convince me that I "need" a new item, I needn't be swayed. How important will that be in the future? The thrill of buying is short-lived.

By putting things and money into perspective, we can help our Christian sister or brother in several ways. We will have more to share, but also, we will not encourage a spirit of coveteousness on their part.

2. *Making a family financial plan.* Having recognized God's authority over our money, we were now ready to make a plan. When my husband proposed that we make a budget, I thought, "Fine. We'll sit down and in a few hours have a neat piece of paper to solve our problems." The solution was not so simple.

First, we read aloud to each other a little book entitled *How to Succeed with Your Money* by George M. Bowman (Chicago: Moody Press). This took several days. Next we kept an exact account of our spending. During this time of keeping track we established what was important to us. We determined with our heads what we wanted to happen with our money. We began by taking Mr. Bowman's general guidelines for a budget. It goes as follows: From your total income, taxes will automatically be taken out. Next determine what proportion you wish to put directly back into the Lord's work. (Ten percent may be a good place to begin.) This will go to the local church and other ministries. The remaining money is what we may budget, making up 100 percent.

Mr. Bowman proposes that the budget be divided like this: Ten percent of the amount we budget becomes "untouchable" savings. General living expenses account for 70 percent of the budget. The remaining 20 percent is the buffer fund. This may be applied to paying past debts, or covering emergencies. Hopefully, the buffer fund will not be needed indefinitely and will also become money designated for special ministries.

Our greatest challenge came in filing down our general expenses to fit its 70 percent. From our detailed records of what we had spent, we established what we thought would be adequate amounts for areas such as clothing, food, and household expenses. When we discovered that they exceeded our designated proportion, we could have given up. But then we could have continued to be run by money rather than vice versa. So we chiseled some more.

We spent six weeks establishing our plan. This may sound like quite a time investment, but it has been well worth the effort. First, we are able to give regularly, as we desire. Secondly, we, especially Bob, no longer are pressured by budget frustrations. We feel a sense of security in knowing how much will be spent for what. We make fewer spur-of-the-moment decisions—which often tend to be impulsive and present-directed rather than future-directed. Thirdly, our money goes farther. Before we had a plan, we could seldom spend a weekend away together. We never had "enough money." Now we include that as a part of our entertainment budget. Because it is important to us, money is set aside for that.

Your budget will be different from anyone else's. But it is important that you have a plan. It's easier to spend less when the satisfaction of managing your money is growing.

After we arrived at a workable plan, we made up a sheet to help us keep records. In addition, we have a little book in which we record all expenditures. At the end of every month we sit down together and take inventory. If we've exceeded our amount in an area one month, we have to cut back the next. We analyze our budget and make revisions every year.

There may be a time when we will not have to

102 / Discover Your Worth

NEFFS, INC.

Month _____ Year _____

INCOME SOURCES	Gross	Net		TITHE
Totals				Other _____
				Total _____

	Monthly		New Total	Interest Earned
SAVINGS				

LIVING EXPENSE	Monthly Actual	Budget	Months + Difference −	Accumulative + Difference −
Mortgage				
Heat - gas				
Telephone				
Electricity				
Water				
Repairs & Cleaning				
Medical				
Life Insurance				
Transportation				
Auto Insurance				
Stamps & paper				
Baby-sitting				
Clothes				
Drycleaning				
Food				
Books, etc.				
Gifts				
Recreation				
Household				
Miscellaneous				

	Monthly		Total	Interest Earned
DEBTS & BUFFER				

Expenses

Total in Account _____

keep daily records of expenditures, but for now we are helped by this discipline.

Neffs, Inc.

We have experienced a side blessing since beginning Neffs, Inc. We have located sources for purchasing most items (including groceries) at a discount. I should not be surprised by this. God is more interested in our success than we are. He wants an abundant life for us. He has promised "many times as much at this time and in the age to come, eternal life" (Luke 18:30).

You may be thinking at this point that being a money manager is difficult. It is, initially. But may I personally assure you that the result will be well worth the effort. It's similar to dieting. The first few days are misery but it's so nice when the scales don't creak when you climb on.

I learned many interesting things about my husband in those six weeks of establishing our budget. I know how many pairs of socks he needs a year. I know the cost of men's dress shoes. I understand his feelings about money.

A major source of conflict has been removed. "No one can serve two masters; for either he will hate the one and love the other, or he will hold to one and despise the other. You cannot serve God and mammon" (Matt. 6:24).

But primarily, the Lord has been given the position He should have in another area of our lives. "Your heavenly Father knows that you need all these things. But seek first His kingdom and His righteousness; and all these things shall be added to you" (Matt. 6:32-33).

8.
Children: A Welcome Legacy

"Children are an heritage of the Lord; and the fruit of the womb is His reward. As arrows are in the hand of a mighty man, so are children of the youth" (Ps. 127:3-4, KJV).

Rejection wears many faces, all of them contorted, most of them covered by a mask. A little girl comes out of her room in the morning. "Good morning, Bert." The greeting sounds normal, even cheery. The little girl responds, "Good morning, Daddy."

But inside, the cancer of rejection is growing. She wants to say, "Daddy, my name isn't Bert. I'm Karen." She is too young to know how deadly the disease is. In her little mind, she apologizes to her father for not being the son he wanted. She resolves to gain his approval by becoming all the things a son would be.

Karen studies and achieves. Years pass. As an attractive teenage girl, she feels ugly. She wants approval to an extreme, especially from boys. She is not closely supervised, has no hours, no restrictions. There are no discussions with her parents about careers, men, politics, or feelings—or anything.

Underneath the clutter of teenage years—friends, art classes, make-up, clothes, dates, books, and schedule—grows a tentacle of rejection: an obsession with pleasing her father.

Tonight she mounts the podium to give the valedictory speech for her high school graduation. She has achieved. Now her father will notice. He must see her. She searches his face, but he doesn't look at her. He is thinking of something else.

The speech is over. Peers and acquaintances congratulate her, but nothing is said at home. Rejection.

College scholarships make possible an expanded world for Karen to search out someone who approves of her. In a whirl of studies, activities, sorority rush, and dates, it seems the cancer has been arrested. Not so. It is only dormant. Well-hidden under hurts and bruises, a new tentacle takes root and grows. *Rebellion.*

Phi Beta Kappa initiates and their parents are invited to meet the president of the college. Would that impress Karen's dad? It is safer not to ask. She goes alone.

Soon she decides which young man will become her husband. Daddy does not approve of him, doesn't ask him about his studies or his career. Daddy doesn't even know him. This isn't surprising. He doesn't know Karen either.

Daddy dictates how the marriage ceremony will be and where. Karen doesn't know that her intense feelings of dislocation and distaste are because inwardly she is standing up and saying, "No, Daddy," while outwardly going through a charade of pleasing him.

The master's degree in Business Administration leads to a prestigious career beginning in a large corporation. Karen receives an infrequent letter from Mom, sometimes a carbon of what is sent to all the family.

A 30-year-old woman lies in bed, sobbing uncontrollably. The full realization has moved in that she can never gain her father's approval. Dark hopelessness covers like a cloud.

What *would* please her father? What and who have gained his admiration in the past? The realization is a gray, smothering blanket. The sickening gray of reality is more painful than the black of not knowing.

Karen's dad is impressed by money and whatever else can boost his ego. She can provide neither and is overcome with nausea. Hatred replaces the anxiety of rejection, and intensifies as she relives years of wishing she were not a woman; recalls relationships with men to prove herself and then get even with men; understands how she has held her husband at a distance, afraid of being rejected if held close.

The hurts and failures all tumble in around her. Psychologists tell us that a person rejected by parents will never recover. However, there is a beautiful verse in the Bible that speaks of the heavenly Father who is not bound by human restrictions and weaknesses. "When my father and my mother forsake me, then the Lord will take me up" (Ps. 27:10, KJV).

For Karen, God has done that in every sense. As a broken and hurting person, she crawled into His lap and sensed His arms holding the fragments of herself, and putting them back together.

Gentleness and love were what she felt in God's

touch, and reassurance that *He* wanted her to be a woman. There was a gentle molding of her misshapen emotions so that she can now give in a freer way than ever before. The freedom to be vulnerable is exhilarating. The delights of a carefree childhood that she missed have opened up, and now she is able to enjoy them with an intense pleasure that a child cannot feel.

At first, Karen could not love her father. But God moved into her inability and loved her father through her till she actually began to feel again for him. It was not the uneasy "how can I please you?" feeling, but a genuine concern for his welfare. It was a new insight into his person and his relationship with Karen's mother. She felt compassion, not resentment.

Karen never confronted her father with the hurts. In his last years he was an aging man who knew he had failed in acquiring most of what had been important to him, and who played on his family's sympathies by admitting that he was ill—physically, emotionally, and psychologically. And it didn't really matter anymore to confront him. Karen had received so much from the hand and heart of her heavenly Father. There was life to be lived, not a score to be evened.

Living Legacy

Children are a gift from the Lord, a legacy, an inheritance. This is a foreign concept today. Abortion statistics show us what so many think of these gifts from the Lord. It is predicted that, through abortion, more than 1,000,000 human gifts from the loving hand of our Lord will be rejected this year in the United States. Many more babies will be born but rejected for a lifetime. Child abuse will rise, and day-care centers will burst at the seams with "gifts" who are not as precious to their parents as paychecks. What was God's intention in giving us these eternal bundles?

Inheritance

Another word for gift is heritage or inheritance. This brings an important focus to the matter of children. When the Bible was being written, *inheritance* had a different meaning from our present-day idea. Today, we connect an inheritance with the death of the person who possessed and willed the property. We think of inheriting *things*, rather than qualities and personhood.

In David's time, a person became an heir at the moment of his birth, while his father was alive. In Roman jurisprudence, the father lives on forever in his family. When he is physically absent, he is spiritually present, not so much *with* as *in* his children.

Let's apply that to Psalm 127:3. Our children are to be representatives from God to our household. They contain the potential for godly characteristics as instilled by their heavenly Father. Each is given a particular bent or personality by his Maker. "Train up a child in the way he should go" (Prov. 22:6). This phrase refers to his particular character that God has uniquely shaped.

The Hebrew inheritance had another characteristic. Land which the Children of Israel received from God was to remain the inalienable property of the family. It was not to be transferred from the proper line of heirs.

Similarly, we are entrusted with children from

God. They are His, not ours, because He is still living (and always will be). It is the spiritual right of our children to live and grow and mature as heirs of God, not of the world. Our position in relationship to our children is that of stewards.

The four little people in our household are heirs of God. This realization is awesome to me. God has allowed me to see a part of Himself through these children whom He has placed under the joint stewardship of Bob and me.

Our family consists of two children born to us and two adopted children. This is a daily example to me of God's grace. God will put into our family whatever child He wishes to have there. He is sovereign. We have prayed for each child. Our children are miracles in the sense that all new life is created only by God. God worked some additional miracles to bring our third child safely into the world.

Before we received each of our adopted sons, we prayed that God would protect them. We prayed that God would direct the individuals making decisions about their care. We prayed that He would prepare our family for the new arrival. In the unique ways that our children have arrived, we are intensely aware of one fact: *God has placed them.* We cannot help but acknowledge that they are His, not ours.

Chosen People

Our family reminds me of my position as a Gentile believer. God's chosen people, the Jews, had been given special promises because of their relationship to Him. As a Gentile, I have been grafted into the family tree by my Saviour, Jesus Christ.

Because of this, I am now heir to all of God's promises and chosen by Him.

Paul, writing to the Romans, reminded them of God's words spoken through Hosea, "I will call those who were not My people, 'My people,' and her who was not beloved, 'Beloved.' And it shall be that in the place where it was said to them, 'You are not My people,' there they shall be called 'sons of the living God'" (Rom. 9:25-26).

Our adopted children are a beautiful illustration of this truth to me. God has grafted them into our family tree. We love them fully as much as the children born into our family. They have all the privileges (and responsibilities) of being a part of the Neff household. They benefit by being supported in the same way as our other children. Their position in our will is equal. They are given the same guidelines for behavior. Through our children, God has taught me more of His heart.

Parent-Stewards

My position in relationship to my children is that of a steward. In a Roman family, a child would be turned over to a teacher for training purposes. That person carried the responsibility of the child's upbringing. Did he determine the characteristics the child was to develop? No. He followed the objectives of the father.

There are three qualifications that parent-stewards must possess. They must (1) know God's objectives; (2) be willing to be God's instruments; (3) and be faithful.

> "And you shall love the Lord your God with all your heart and with

all your soul and with all your might. And these words, which I am commanding you today, shall be on your heart; and you shall teach them diligently to your sons and shall talk of them when you sit in your house and when you walk by the way and when you lie down and when you rise up" (Deut. 6:5-7).

God's Objectives for Children

We, as Christian parents, receive our behavioral objectives for our children from God. This is easily said, but extremely difficult to live. It is my natural tendency to want to choose goals for my children based on what would please me.

I enjoy watching wrestling. This sport requires more self-discipline than most athletic events. A corner of my heart can visualize one of our sons wrestling in the Olympics. But I must acknowledge that God may not have that in His objectives for any of our sons. Yes, I can and must direct them toward worthwhile activities. But my objective must be to build godly mature men, not to satisfy Mama's whims.

What are some of God's objectives for the children He has placed under our stewardship? His first objective is that Valerie, John, Charles, and Robby know and accept His Son. God wants to spend eternity with each child He has placed under your stewardship. It is primarily your responsibility that your child accept Christ's sacrifice for his sins, so that he can spend eternity with his heavenly Father. How it must grieve our Lord to see parents setting examples that exclude these little ones from an eternity with the One who can love and care for them as no one else can.

Another objective we receive from God for our children is that they develop Christlike character. A part of this character is truthfulness. "Do not let kindness and truth leave you; bind them around your neck, write them on the tablet of your heart. So you will find favor and good repute in the sight of God and man" (Prov. 3:3-4).

Another Christlike characteristic is obedience. "He who has My commandments and keeps them, he it is who loves Me; and he who loves Me shall be loved by My Father, and I will love him, and will disclose Myself to him" (John 14:21). A child's first lessons in obedience to his heavenly Father should come through the loving hands of his parents.

Christlike character includes love. "Little children, let us not love with word or with tongue, but in deed and truth. We shall know by this that we are of the truth, and shall assure our heart before Him" (1 John 3:18-19).

Parents in the Spotlight

Our first question is usually, "How can we teach all this to our children?" The answer is simple. By example. The spotlight is on you and me.

Perhaps this is the cause for so many rejected children. Being in the spotlight can be extremely uncomfortable. It's easier to ignore or reject our little gifts than examine ourselves and begin the stretching experience of becoming the example we need to be.

Parents are to know God and His Word. How can we aim for God's objectives if we do not know them? We must be addicted to studying God. It is true that children are in the position of learners. As teachers we should have more knowledge, wisdom, and understanding than our children, so that we can lead them. However, we can never feel that we have arrived. We must be continually growing and learning ourselves.

As a high school counselor, I tutored a student with terminal cancer. In addition to his physical problems, he was emotionally immature. After meeting his mother, I knew why. As we sat in her living room, talking, she became very excited and upset over the fact that her cigarette had burned down in her fingers and she had no ash tray. She began screaming at her children to bring ash trays. After several minutes of turmoil and commotion, the crisis was resolved by a dirty coffee cup. There was no example of emotional maturity in that home for Dave to follow.

We cannot take our children farther than we have grown ourselves. This should stimulate us to begin a growth spurt!

God's Instruments

We must be willing to be God's instruments. It is no new revelation that children require unselfish giving on the part of their parent-stewards. We learned in an earlier chapter how our emotional tanks are filled so that we can give.

This principle explains why there is so much failure in raising children today. Adults who are unsure of their own identity and have no spiritual resources can give only to a limited extent. This will be true of all adults who do not have an intimate relationship with Christ as their personal

Saviour. Unfortunately, it is also true of some Christian adults who have not drawn on their spiritual resources and discovered their unique position as God's children.

Stability

Being God's instruments requires that we put aside our own desires. We are pressed in our culture to believe that we must float along with our personal ups and downs and succumb to circumstances. A recent best-seller, *Passages*, is an example of this notion. It categorizes crisis periods through which we all "must" pass. An underlying theory is that no structure can last more than seven or eight years. The author states, "we must be willing to change chairs if we want to grow. There is no permanent compatibility between a chair and a person. And there is no one right chair" (Gail Sheehy, *Passages*, New York: Bantam Books).

If we internalize this worldly philosophy, we cannot become the parents God wants us to be. Parenthood requires stability, maturity. We have already seen that God intends the marriage partnership to be permanent. He also intends that our life pattern be permanent. And He is that life pattern.

Decision-making

A person floating up and down with circumstances does not make decisions. Children need decision-making parents. Children develop security knowing what is expected of them, what freedoms they now have and those they must earn later. Decision-making requires active involvement with our chil-

Children: A Welcome Legacy / 115

dren. We must spend time with them and know what is happening in their lives in order to make good decisions. We must know the content of their school courses. We must know the activities of the clubs and programs they attend. We need to know the sponsors and their life-styles. As parents we need to be acquainted with their friends. This consumes time and emotional energy.

Time Commitment

We cannot be God's instruments if we spend little or no time with our children.

One young mother found her fulfillment in a job which required that she be away from home 7:00 A.M. till 4:00 P.M. She had one child in grammar school and one preschooler at the time. She discovered that her job required so much energy, both physical and emotional, that she could not enjoy her own children in the evening. She found a creative alternative: night school. Attending classes three nights a week was easier than "enjoying" her children.

Because she spent little time with her husband during the week, she concentrated on going places with him during the weekends.

Five years of this brought about predictable behavior from her children. They sense rejection. They show this by telling her they don't like her and by displaying their worst behavior when she arrives home. They are undisciplined. The succession of baby-sitters has not instilled in them consistent guidelines for behavior. Therefore, they resent authority. Their most consistent companion has been the television. Can we expect secure, well-adjusted children from uninvolved parents?

No. Our example in Deuteronomy shows children as an integral part of the daily activities of the parents. This is an extreme antithesis to our nursery school, baby-sitter-oriented society!

By now you may feel I am unsympathetic toward a mother's need (and father's too) for time that is not intensely child-oriented. Not true. I must be an adequate person before I can be an adequate parent.

My adequacy begins in the quiet dark when I read and pray. This is not a child-oriented time. As I mentioned earlier, there are times when Bob and I plan to be away from our brood. The areas that God has given me for ministry are not child-oriented. (I'm especially thankful for this.)

There are changes we've made in our household in order to enjoy our children more when we're together. Our home is decorated with small children in mind. Dark carpeting and washable wallpaper and paint help us enjoy them all the more. I have temporarily laid aside crafts that would make me irritable with my children. If I am concentrating on a complicated crewel pattern, the normal interruptions of children become nerve-wracking and I begin to think of how quickly I could do the task if they weren't around. I know it is not God's intention that I resent my children's presence. So crewel is set aside for rare occasions such as travel times. Maybe such needlework will fit in at another life-stage.

Shaping with Love

An instrument of God is used to shape something—in this case—somebody. The primary medium through which we shape our children is love. Somehow, we have misplaced the emphasis in parent-child relationships. We have put the primary emphasis on discipline in the negative sense of punishment. It is true that our children are to obey us. But they can learn to obey us best through our loving instruction and constructive discipline. "And fathers, do not provoke your children to anger; but bring them up in the discipline and instruction of the Lord" (Eph. 6:4).

Excessive punishment of a child will certainly provoke wrath. Titus 2:4 tells us we are to love our children. One of the greatest results of a loving parent-child relationship is that the child will want to imitate our example. How much easier training becomes! What will be the result of a godly, loving parent? An eager imitator following her/his footsteps. This concept can either make our parent role much easier, or frighten us. The difference depends on our relationship to and dependence on God.

Remember that loving your child means that you follow the behavioral characteristics set down in 1 Corinthians 13. Having a warm, emotional feeling for them is not enough. That should not be called love. It certainly doesn't provide the strength to carry you through times when children are ill or going through emotional turmoil and your household seems up for grabs. At those times you must have the kind of compassion that consistently keeps doing what you know is best for them even though you see few results.

Faithfulness

The third requirement of a steward is faithfulness. "Let a man so account of us, as of the ministers of Christ, and stewards of the mysteries of God.

Moreover it is required in stewards, that a man be found faithful. . . . He that judgeth me is the Lord" (1 Cor. 4:1-2, 4, KJV).

We are faithful because we are placed in a stewardship position over God's property. It does seem to me that children are a part of the mystery of God. It is a mystery that in a little bundle of seven pounds of complete dependence, there is the potential to affect the world. It is a mystery that this little being who can only cry is designed to satisfy God's heart by giving Him fellowship and devotion.

Though a little child is a mystery in many ways, he unlocks many of God's mysteries. The child is an illustration of faith that believes beyond external circumstances.

We are to become as children in living our faith. How is a child characterized? By activity—by involvement. Children are not spectators by nature. Whatever is happening, they want to do too. They want to play baseball with people twice their size, paint from the highest ladder. Our faith is to result in involvement.

As we exercise our stewardship with our children, what is our goal? Too often, we want the approval of Aunt Nel, or the neighborhood women, or our boss. First Corinthians 4:4 makes it very clear that our work will be examined by our Lord. Our objective should be to please Him.

Can We Reject God's Gifts?

We have no precedent in Scripture for rejecting gifts from God. In fact, to reject a gift from God is to reject Him. Are we so wise that we know better than God what we should have? "Every

Children: A Welcome Legacy / 119

good thing bestowed and every perfect gift is from above, coming down from the Father of lights, with whom there is no variation, or shifting shadow" (James 1:17).

God in His wisdom gave to Bob and me precisely the children He intended us to have. Two (and possibly a blossoming third) qualify as "strong-willed" children, at least by Dr. James Dobson's definition (*The Strong-Willed Child*, Wheaton: Tyndale House Publishers, Inc.).

Perhaps we would have chosen more compliant, easily molded gifts. But they are God's *good* gifts to us. God matched their characters to what He knew would be best for us. (Gasp!)

We must be careful not to base final judgment on the unfinished product. Only God can keep the complete record of our stewardship. I claim 2 Timothy 1:12 for my children: "But I am not ashamed; for I know whom I have believed and I am convinced that He is able to guard what I have entrusted to Him until that day."

After I have been faithful in what I know to do, I am still overwhelmed with my own inadequacy. But God is big enough to take my little efforts with my precious children and keep them. He can put His hedge about my children and guard them where I cannot go. He can guide their minds from forces I cannot detect. Beyond the sphere of the parent-steward, God is.

9.
Reach Out

As Christians placed here on Planet Earth, we have a job to do beyond our families and personal interests. We are to be the salt of the earth. We are to witness of Jesus to the world. We are to minister to others. The ways we are to minister are as varied as the needs and hurts of people. The Christian family is the training ground, the growing place, a home base; but it is not an end in itself.

We need a concept of balance in this area. We cannot neglect our families and homes. Neither can we become so ingrown, looking out for only our immediate family, that we do not see the world in its deteriorating condition.

How Do We Minister?

What guidelines does Scripture set for ministering? First, we are to be vessels through whom Christ loves others. This sounds so easy, but it is the most difficult command in Scripture. To live it is to grow beyond what is easy and comfortable for us.

Regardless of what attention-getting gimmicks

we use, our words and actions are useless without love. "If I speak with the eloquence of men and of angels, but have no love, I become no more than blaring brass or crashing cymbal. If I have the gift of foretelling the future and hold in my mind not only all human knowledge but the very secrets of God, and if I also have that absolute faith which can move mountains, but have no love, I amount to nothing at all. If I dispose of all that I possess, yes, even if I give my own body to be burned, but have no love, I achieve precisely nothing (1 Cor. 13:1-3, PH).

How much "ministering" goes on today that would not stand the test of these verses? Love is the difference between philanthropic good deeds and Christian ministering.

Go back to chapter 5 and reread the behavioral characteristics of love. These characteristics describe our attitude as we minister. Without these we may as well save our energy.

When we have filled our storehouse of love from God's Word we are ready to minister. How do we do it? A beautiful observation I have made of Christian ministering is that it follows no stereotype. No wonder! Look at our Example. Jesus' activities of ministering were as varied as the people to whom He reached.

In one place we see Him ministering to psychological needs. In other places, He fed them physically or dealt with their physical illnesses. His activities were bathed in prayer. Read John 17. He interceded with His heavenly Father for their (and our) spiritual needs. Repeatedly He left the people to get alone and pray. "And when He had sent the multitudes away, He went up into a mountain apart to pray; and when the evening was come,

He was there alone" (Matt. 14:23, KJV). "He went out into a mountain to pray and continued all night in prayer to God" (Luke 6:12, KJV). The effectiveness of our tiny efforts at ministering can be multiplied by bathing them in prayer. It is easier to have a loving spirit when we have prayed and are in an attitude of prayer as we minister.

Have you ever served dinner to a large number of people? You begin with enthusiasm and great gusto. Then something goes wrong in the kitchen—maybe the oven timer—which has never worked well before—decided to turn off the oven *permanently*. I have had this experience, and it wasn't funny at the time! My attitude of service and optimism began to dwindle.

But an attitude of prayer carries one through those circumstances. "Lord, I committed this dinner to you and the oven is yours too. You must have a neighbor with a functioning oven or a topic of conversation for us while the potatoes boil on the stove and the roast migrates to the electric skillet." When we commit our efforts at ministering to the Lord, it is more difficult for us to fume over details.

Second Sight

As Christians, we have a special advantage in helping people. We can detect needs that non-Christians do not notice. As we grow with the Lord we become more sensitive to others' feelings and problems.

We see an example of this in the Philippian jailer in Acts 16. Paul and Silas were placed in his custody after they had been badly beaten. He put them in stocks, in a high security part of the prison. During the night, despite their raw backs, Paul and Silas prayed and sang praises to God. God intervened for them by sending an earthquake which shook the prison till all the doors were opened and the prisoners freed. The jailer, awaking to find his charges free, prepared to take his life. It would be demanded of him by his superiors for doing such a sloppy job. But Paul stopped him. There, in that prison, the jailer became a follower of Jesus. "And he took them that very hour of the night and washed their wounds (Acts 16:33).

Were the backs of Paul and Silas cut and bleeding when the jailer put them in stocks? Yes, but he was insensitive to their hurt. Christ transformed him to a person of compassion.

When Others Hurt, We Should Too

Have we as a Christian community become callous to the hurts of our fellow humans? That is not God's intention. We are told to love one another (1 John 3:11). This is not a passive love, but an active love that reaches out, to hurting people with soothing actions and help.

We should hurt to hear of old people in nursing homes who have not had visitors for months. Do you feel you are not a brilliant conversationalist? You can breathe and walk and smile and read. That is sufficient equipment for reaching out to a lonely old person.

We should hurt to hear of children who must be cared for in places where there are too few hands to dispense hugs and kisses as well as sandwiches and tissues. These places would be empty if Christian families adopted or became foster parents for these children.

We should hurt to hear of couples who are splitting. Sometimes all we can do is hurt and pray—and that is valuable. Sometimes we can make a phone call and express our concern and availability for companionship. Divorce is lonely.

We cannot know of the hurts of the world if we are hibernating in our Christian family or serving only in our local church. These places are refueling grounds, shelters where we bring anyone and everyone who needs God's love.

Open Your Home and Your Heart

It should not surprise us to see throughout Scripture that God wants us to be hospitable. God has a big heart. He wants our hearts to be enlarged. "He executes justice for the orphan and the widow, and shows His love for the alien by giving him food and clothing. So show your love for the alien, for you were aliens in the land of Egypt" (Deut. 10:18-19).

From the Old Testament through the New we see instructions for opening up our selves, our hearts and our possessions to other people. "Be hospitable to one another without complaint" (1 Peter 4:9). Interestingly, this verse is sandwiched between a verse on love and one on being good stewards of the grace we've received from God.

Priscilla and Aquila

One of the most effective ministries of hospitality described in the Bible was performed by Paul's tentmaking friends, Priscilla and Aquila. Their hospitality encompassed both church and home—a branch of the church met in their home. We also know that Paul was their houseguest when he arrived in Corinth after leaving Athens. They had just moved there from Rome, but whether or not they were completely settled didn't matter. They were hospitable because Paul needed their hospitality.

Priscilla and Aquila had at least two areas of common interest. They were both tentmakers by trade and both were knowledgeable in the Word and in the Spirit. They were Paul's traveling companions from Corinth to Ephesus. We see them in Ephesus educating Apollos, not by contradicting him or asking him embarrassing questions in front of the crowd, but by taking him aside and teaching him. This is an example of teamwork in trade, in hospitality, and in teaching.

Priscilla and Aquila were happy to serve behind the scenes. Being hospitable does not bring recognition from people like sizable contributions do. But for eternity, Priscilla and Aquila are held before us as examples of a godly husband and wife team.

Why Is Hospitality Hard?

Why do we, as a Christian community, find it hard to be hospitable? Why do we become ingrown? The reason is that we are allowing ourselves to be conformed to this world.

Francis A. Schaeffer points out that the majority of people have adopted two values: *personal peace* and *affluence*. "Personal peace means just to be let alone, not to be troubled by the troubles of other people, whether across the world or across the city. Personal peace means wanting to have my personal life pattern undisturbed in my lifetime.

Affluence means an overwhelming and ever-increasing prosperity—a life made up of things, things, and more things" (*Moody Monthly*, "Humanism, A Threat to Your Liberty," February 1978).

Both of these worldly values have crept into our Christian experience. Both are incongruous with hospitality.

Personal peace is certainly disturbed when we are sensitive to other people. Our phones ring more. Our days of leisure become days of serving, maybe cleaning someone else's home. Our private coffee corners in our kitchens become crowded with people needing listeners. Our neat cast-iron schedules must become flexible to allow for the unexpected, to make room for the "stranger" passing through.

Our affluence is certainly affected by hospitality. Our cars roll over more miles, our grocery cupboards empty faster, our tablecloths wear out sooner. Our carpets get traffic patterns. Our tightly clasped fists that shout "Mine" have to be opened. Our accumulated furniture and lawn supplies must be labeled "Owned by God, operated by me."

Our hospitality extends to whomever the Lord sends. We know that He was no respecter of persons. His invitation is "whosoever will." Our invitations tend to include "whoever I'm comfortable with", or "whoever will complement me." This is being a respecter of persons.

You may say, "But I have no common ground with that person. How can I relate to her?" or "What interests do we share?"

Look at Paul's policy. "Yes, whatever a person is like, I try to find common ground with him, so that he will let me tell him about Christ and let

Christ save him (1 Cor. 9:22b, LB). Pray for the Lord to show you your common ground with whomever He brings into your life.

Learn to ask questions. Listen carefully. The Lord will faithfully answer your prayer. He desires your growth in hospitality more than you do!

Why do some people seem to be showered with opportunities to be hospitable? Perhaps God has found them to be faithful with what opportunities and material supplies they have. We need more hospitable families.

We Learn by Giving

There are endless lessons we learn from hospitality. Our world becomes bigger as we meet varied people and we hear of their experiences. Our husbands and children learn to give as they see our willingness to serve. We reap what we sow. Paul tells us why he makes an effort to find common ground. "I do this to get the Gospel to them and also for the blessing I myself receive when I see them come to Christ" (1 Cor. 9:23, LB).

Hospitality also can "encourage the fainthearted, help the weak" (1 Thes. 5:14). How refreshing to laugh together over a common meal and feel the warmth of acceptance. We experience these rewards when we are hospitable. But that is not our motivation. Our motivation is to obey God's direction to us. The satisfaction from obedience is motivation enough.

Pride Makes Us Afraid

Practicing hospitality requires that I lay aside my pride. Opening our lives and homes to others means that they will see us under varied circumstances. When someone lives at the Neff residence for awhile, he/she learns that our children do not always stay clean. Their table manners are far from perfect. Our regular menus are not exotic. They learn that, without cosmetics, the lady of the house has dark circles under her eyes. They learn that clutter mounts rapidly in our household. (I wonder why no one has invented a toy vacuum—one big enough to slurp up large objects.)

Are we afraid that people may learn that we are only growing Christians, not spiritual giants?

The foundation for much entertaining (not hospitality) is pride. Our work will be tried by fire. Building a foundation of pride is like building from straw. When the quality of our work is tried by fire, it will be burned up. There is no reward for all the effort when the foundation is pride. Pride means we are focusing on ourselves. Will it help my image if I serve my best gourmet meal? Will people leave thinking *I'm* the perfect hostess? Will people marvel at *my* abilities?

We cannot be focusing on the needs of our guests if we are concentrating on "How will I look?" We cannot be sensitive to how we can best serve them.

Pride makes us upset if something flops. Pride makes us self-conscious and ill at ease around strangers. "For who regards you as superior? And what do you have that you did not receive? But if you did receive it, why do you boast as if you had not received it?" (1 Cor. 4:7)

"God is opposed to the proud, but gives grace to the humble" (James 4:6). Realizing that all I am and have I received from God, I give back to Him my abilities for His use. He uses me, then, for ministering.

Do You Want to Share Your Home?

Is Christian hospitality a new area for you? Study Scripture on hospitality to become acquainted with God's objectives. Tell God that you are available for that ministry. Then prepare practically to become more at ease.

I find it helpful to keep on hand the ingredients of an easy casserole. I never have to wonder what the surprise menu will be. We have a favorite pumpkin bread at our house. I like to have some frozen; it becomes a dessert with tea in the evening or a coffee cake in the morning. Are these little preparations necessary? No. But they may give you confidence if you are beginning to open your home.

Having studied God's Word and made yourself available, you will not have to wait long to be used! Bob and I prayed one morning that our Lord would make 1 Peter 4:9 real to us. That day the phone rang; a woman from another country had flown in to O'Hare. The people she expected to meet her were not there. She got our phone number from a flier and called to see if we could help. Within the hour she was settled into our home. Nine weeks later she left for another city. In her stay she attended Bible seminars and sat in on Bible classes. An added bonus was that for one and a half weeks our household included two additional children. (That made a six-year-old, two three-year-olds, and two one-year-olds.) It was a rich experience for all of us. We learned, among other things, that God uses our availability—quickly.

Our objective in ministering is to reach out and serve other people. Who can calculate the good that has been accomplished through the ages with

Christian hospitality, to name only one way of ministering.

Serve and Be Enriched

But there is another very important benefit of ministering. Serving is therapy, emotional and spiritual, for our individual lives.

We observe the increase in emotional illness in women. Depression is the enemy of Christian and non-Christian alike. Many cases of depression would never occur if we were actively seeking ways to serve outside our little worlds. Depression often begins with a "poor me" attitude. "Look at my needs." "Isn't my life miserable?" We effectively combat these tendencies when we get our eyes off of ourselves and look beyond the sphere of our little family. Our life assumes balance when we are in touch with others.

Sometimes, our problems seem smaller, but even if they don't, there is a healing that accompanies ministry. As Christians, we have a need to give. Serving satisfies that need.

To what extreme do we go in ministering? Many are afraid they will be taken advantage of. That is a very real possibility but it does not mean we are free *not* to serve. We do not lack for examples in Scripture. Look at Christ first. Did people "take advantage" of Him? No doubt they did. He had little privacy. It appears that one of the few times He could pray alone was during the night hours because His days were filled with serving. He had no home or material wealth that He had accumulated for Himself, no circle from which He excluded other people.

What was the result of this self-sacrifice? Did

he have devoted followers? When Jesus' followers should have supported Him most, they bickered about who was the greatest among them, and then considered leaving Him.

Ministry Costs and Pays

Paul lists what he endured because of the ministry to which God had called him. Second Corinthians 11:23 tells us of sacrifices he made and pain that he endured to carry out what he knew God wanted of him. After reading that list, the little we sacrifice for ministry looks meager in comparison. I have only experienced one of those 26 hardships. And the tiny amount of weariness could not compare to Paul's.

With all those physical demands and hardships, he carried the weight of the baby churches he had founded. He felt with them. This drained him of energy to a greater extent than any amount of physical labor.

We must be careful not to absorb the world's "don't get involved" attitude. We have no choice but to risk hurts and being taken advantage of when we determine to follow Christ.

Once we have known the joy of serving we will be discontent with a life lacking involvement. "But Jesus said to him, 'No one, after putting his hand to the plow and looking back, is fit for the kingdom of God'" (Luke 9:62).

If our ministry is in the flesh we will be happy for a break, a time to rest. If our ministry is in spiritual partnership with God, following Christ's example, energized by the Holy Spirit, we will thrive on serving and be discontent with idleness.

10.
Planned Neglect

What dictates your calendar? One mother's schedule is dominated by a part-time job. And her children's schedules are determined by her job and the resulting change in sleep schedule. The children may come home from school and see a note on the door that says, "Don't come in the house till 5:30. I'm sleeping."

How disappointing to know that Mommy's spending money and sleep are more important than the people in her life, especially when you're the "people."

You tell others what is important to you by what you do with each hour. The clock and calendar are like the scrambled arms of an octopus that need to be in swimming order. We can either use them efficiently, as if we had eight arms and legs, or be strangled by them.

First Priority

The most important priority in conquering clock and calendar is spending time with the Lord, communicating with Him through Scripture and prayer.

Having studied my Bible in the small hours of the morning, prayed, and organized my verse cards for memorization during the day, I should be guaranteed a day of complete victory. Right? I wish we could shout an assured, "Right." But life is referred to as a battle (1 Tim. 6:12; 2 Tim. 4:7). And it will be till we are in God's presence.

Not long ago, I was preparing to begin teaching a new Bible class. I bubbled with excitement over the new opportunity to share. The chapter I had chosen to begin with was especially stimulating. I was off and running, assured of God's blessing.

But the night before the new class was not so bubbly! I returned home late from finishing a Bible study series. Our infant son couldn't keep his formula down. He fretted uncomfortably. By 12:30 A.M., he was finally able to sleep. Within a few hours he was up again. My husband was out of town so I was the night-duty nurse. By 5:30 A.M. my little bundle was ready to sleep again, but other bedroom floors were squeaking as the older children got up. Our two-year-old Charles' cheery greeting of "Hi, Mommy," sparkled with that "I'm up to face the day" gleam. Self-pity began to seep in. "Poor Miriam. You're serving the Lord. You should be able to face the day without dark circles under your eyes."

The Human Predicament

In this life we are never free from our old nature. We are never free from fleshly lusts. The devil has not given up on Miriam yet. He still knows my weaknesses. I sense an intimate understanding of Paul and his predicament. "For I know that nothing good dwells in me, that is, in my flesh; for the wishing is present in me, but the doing of the good is not. For the good that I wish, I do not do; but I practice the very evil that I do not wish" (Rom. 7:18-19).

This conflict makes studying the Bible priority number one. The conflict also means that, at times, studying the Word will be a painful experience, like pulling back the drapes from winter-weathered windows on a bright spring morning. The sunlight shines through and all the smudges and streaks stand out.

Some mornings, reading the Word is like a fresh, spring rain. It refreshes, revives, and initiates a cleansing growth spurt. Other mornings, it is like a bursting sunrise in the mountains. Immediate questions are answered. Verses that I need for that very day just "happen" to be in the portion of my alloted Scripture that morning.

Some days, the Word of God becomes a mirror reflecting my own failure. My worldliness and unworthiness stand in sharp contrast to Christ's total dedication to glorifying my Heavenly Father. This hurts; but the tears I weep in repentance and rededication are not wasted. God keeps account of my tears (Ps. 56:8), and I am assured that in heaven I will be free from this battle. "And He shall wipe away every tear from their eyes; and there shall no longer be any death; there shall no longer be any mourning, or crying, or pain; the first things have passed away" (Rev. 21:4).

Regardless of whether my time of Bible reading and prayer is exciting and invigorating, or painful and searching, it is essential for me to keep reading daily. For I cannot grow spiritually without studying the Bible regularly and consistently.

First Things First

Our natural inclinations seem to tell us to be consistent in our study of Scripture—if it is convenient, if we perfectly understand what we are reading, and if the passage can have a dramatic application to our lives.

This attitude will not lead to spiritual growth. Fresh insights are often the result of unanswered questions that send us digging for answers. Time with the Lord may be treasured and more fully used when it is chiseled out of an overcrowded schedule. We make our time in the Word with our Lord a priority.

An accomplished violinist was asked to share the secret of her great talent. She answered "Planned neglect." She planned to neglect everything that interfered with her goal of becoming an expert violinist.

We can learn from her discovery. We cannot grow spiritually without planned neglect. "But whatever things were gain to me, those things I have counted as loss for the sake of Christ. More than that, I count all things to be loss in view of the surpassing value of knowing Christ Jesus my Lord, for whom I have suffered the loss of all things, and count them but rubbish in order that I may gain Christ" (Phil. 3:7-8).

How much do I want to be God's woman? To the extent that I will neglect whatever interferes with my intimate relationship with my Lord. Does picking up a women's magazine keep me from studying God? Then I will neglect it and study God first. Perhaps I won't pick up the magazine till it is outdated and perhaps never. No matter. It is not a priority.

I may never window-shop. It isn't important if I

know the latest fads. This is planned neglect. In fact, my battle with materialism may be helped.

Are my hours filled with organizational meetings and phone calls? As good as the projects may be, they are secondary to my relationship with my Lord. God is continually sorting in our lives. He weeds out the good to make room for the better. The better must be replaced with the best: Himself, that we "may be found in Him, . . . may know Him, and the power of His resurrection, and the fellowship of His sufferings, being conformed to His death" (Phil. 3:10).

Lay Aside Encumbrances

Coming to know God is a process of growth. There is no instant formula to acquire it. But we are given all the keys in Scripture. Paul says "forgetting what lies behind and reaching forward to what lies ahead, I press on" (Phil. 3:14). In Hebrews, we learn that we are to "lay aside every encumbrance" (Heb. 12:1).

I find that to "lay aside every encumbrance" means that sometimes I cannot pay attention to things said to me. There are some people who continually sing a "How can you do all that?" theme song. I find it a monotonous melody. What they mean is, "Don't do so much, so I won't look so lazy in comparison." The second verse goes something like this, "With all those small children you must be very busy." Third verse: "You look tired." And so on.

My human reaction to this song is: "My goodness, if no one else is doing what I'm doing, I must be abnormal. I'd better change." Then I begin to think that perhaps my family is to be the full circle of my life. Open doors for ministry are just tantalizing teasers I must reject till everyone's in school. Thirdly, though I felt perfectly fine a minute ago, now my feet ache a bit and my head is a little heavy. I am a bit hungry and I haven't been able to finish a cup of coffee while it was hot since the last time I was in a restaurant.

This kind of encumbrance is indeed heavy and can keep us lagging behind instead of pressing on. But I have found an answer to such remarks: "There are lots of things I don't do." Mentally I add: One of which is looking around to see what other women are doing.

Be God's Woman

Being God's woman is not some kind of "high" that keeps us up permanently. We sometimes paint a rosy, smiling picture to the non-Christian, saying that accepting Christ will make life pleasant and all problems will be resolved immediately. This is untrue and unfair.

But may I share with you what I have found being God's woman to be. First of all, it is right. Because God is who He is, it is right to actively place my life in His hands and expect Him to shape me into whatever He pleases.

Secondly, it is satisfying. Though all our outer conflicts are not visibly resolved, we can have peace that says, "I know where I came from, who I am, and where I'm going." Because these facts are so secure, I can trust God for how I get from here to there.

Thirdly, being God's woman is the most exciting challenge in my life. (Yes, even greater than "richly satisfying" my husband's needs and raising four children!) I will never arrive spiritually before my Lord returns, but it is a most stimulating adventure to be on the way.

Intellectually, my Lord's revelation of Himself in His Word is the most fascinating study. Its scope is broader than any other book. When it has been read and reread, there are still new layers of truth to explore. "Oh, the depth of the riches both of the wisdom and knowledge of God! How unsearchable are His judgments and unfathomable His ways!" (Rom. 11:33)

Emotionally, I expand through my relationship to my Lord. It is His desire that our ability to love extend beyond anything possible to the human without Christ. He makes possible the ability to empathize, to feel with others, to experience compassion beyond our human potential. Through Him we can hold together through great sorrows and difficulties. Becoming more sensitized means we hurt more for other people. But it also means we experience joys that are beyond our comprehension without Christ.

Joanne has five young children. Her husband cannot keep a job. Months pass with no income. Yet Joanne is a good listener. Other people bring their problems to her. She is ready to sit down with a lonely person or encourage a hurting sister by cutting and styling her hair.

How can she carry her own burden and still have emotional stamina to carry another's burden too? She is God's woman. Ten years ago she was self-centered. But through her problems (not in spite of them), she has been stretched to be sensitive to the hurts of others.

Have you ever agonized over a sister's problem till you literally ached for her? Unless your compassion reaches that height, you will never experience the release of tears of peace as you pray and sense God's power over every detail of your friend's problem.

Psychologically, as God's woman you can have your head together. You need not live a yo-yo existence of being up one day and down the next, according to the circumstances. The lordship of Christ in your life will make possible a balance that is becoming rare. This consistency makes life much more pleasant. (To this my husband will shout, "Amen!")

Physically, I recognize that my body's well-being is not a top priority. Though I must not neglect it (it is another of my tools), I will not spend excessive time on "maintenance." As God's woman I do not have time to be a hypochondriac.

Today Belongs to God

To accept salvation through Christ but not accept and pursue growth into becoming God's woman is like sampling the hors d'oeuvres and leaving before the main course. It's like saying "Lord, I'll take the everlasting life, but save the abundant-life-now for someone else. Crawling along the ground is so exciting—why should I experiment with running or even flying like an eagle?"

Being God's woman will not guarantee your financial success, clout in this world, or an always rested body. But who needs those things when you have the joy of the Lord?

"This is the day which the Lord has made; let us rejoice and be glad in it" (Ps. 118:24). This becomes my theme song. Though each day has battles, the victory has been won by Christ. It becomes my challenge to live like I've won the victory.

One of the valuable tools God has given me is time. He tells me to "redeem the time." For each day I have objectives: what needs to happen. I record these in a daily calendar. It includes study time, household tasks, appointments, time with my children, phone calls to be made, and prayer reminders—to name a few things. However, it is not enough that I record what should get done during each day. They must be ordered by priorities. "If I can only accomplish one thing, what should that be?" This becomes priority number one. If my day changes and I cannot achieve what I have determined to do, I will have the peace at the end of the day of knowing the most important thing was done. When asked to take on another activity for a day, I weigh that against the importance of the things already planned. Having done this I can either say No with definiteness or Yes without regrets.

My daily plan is given to the Lord early in the morning. "Lord, it seems like this is what should happen today. Sort out what You don't want and add. It's Your day. Balance the being with the doing." All our beautiful lists and priorities are wasted effort if our attitude is to elevate ourselves and not our Lord. If you need more specific help on setting priorities, you might read Ann Ortlund's book, *Disciplines of the Beautiful Woman*, (Waco, Texas: Word, Inc.).

Say Yes to God

Many women tell me they feel they are on a treadmill of endless activity. Their days are filled with everything but the peace of knowing they are God's woman. The result of all the activity seems to be zero. I always ask the same question. "Are you spending time with the Lord every day?" How sad to hear a negative answer. "How badly do you want to be God's woman?" I am often told that it is hard to say No to requests to do this or support that. I understand. Tape this note over your phone: "Saying Yes now may mean that I am saying No to God."

Unless I am growing with Him I cannot be successful on any of His assignments. I may go through the motions but my success will be due to the arm of the flesh. Then when it is tried by fire it will burn as straw. God cannot add His multiplying blessing to my self-efforts. Under these conditions, even the fullest, most glamorous schedule becomes boring and we feel we are grinding out another day.

Sheri volunteered to organize the church nursery for the year. She knew that her life had become ingrown and she needed to reach out to help others. She began organizing, making charts, phone calls, and scrubbing with extraordinary energy. Her year of service had a beautiful beginning.

Eleven months later, the picture had changed. Sheri was tired of filling in for workers who didn't show up, but she refused to ask for additional help. She felt it was *her* job. She was spiritually starving from having missed worshiping with the body of believers so frequently. She became bitter over carrying a burden that she felt was too big for one person. She was enveloped in martyrdom and self-pity. No one praised her efforts. She had begun in the Spirit and finished in the strength of the arm of the flesh. That's a pretty sorry finish.

At the End of Time

I find it a spiritual tonic to study Old Testament prophecy and John's Book of The Revelation. This reminds me in a fresh way that my world is completely in God's hands. He is working toward His desired objectives even through the decaying process which our world and humankind are experiencing. I see that everything and every person is ultimately in His hands. The blinders around my human eyes are pushed back a bit so that I can see beyond my little world and grasp a bit of God's eternity.

"And they shall see His face and His name shall be on their foreheads. And there shall no longer be any night; and they shall not have need of the light of a lamp nor the light of the sun, because the Lord God shall illumine them; and they shall reign forever and ever" (Rev. 22:4-5).

Then I will no longer wrestle with time to have moments in Bible study "because the Lord God shall illumine" me. I will no longer pray for His direction. "He shall dwell among them, and they shall be His people, and God Himself shall be among them" (Rev. 21:3).

In the meanwhile I claim His promise: "And behold, I am coming quickly. Blessed is he who heeds the words of the prophecy of this Book" (Rev. 22:7).

Amen. Come Lord Jesus.

11.
A Single Person

We are all single at some time in our lives. Perhaps you have never been married. Maybe you are divorced or widowed. You may be married but still feel alone, as you and your husband live in two different worlds. This is true when Christian marries non-Christian. It is also true when two Christians marry, but one matures and the other remains a child spiritually and emotionally. Or when people allow their interests and careers to lead them far apart from one another. Regardless of why you feel alone, this chapter is for you.

We have said that God has unlimited ways in which He'd like to use us All of humankind received gifts, and those given to women are varied. Some gifts are best used by·single people. Others reach their full potential in marriage. Some women have years of both marriage and the single life.

Being Single Is Ok

It is becoming increasingly popular to be single. The marriage rate has been declining since 1972.

Divorce has doubled since 1960. The median age of marriage is getting higher. Being single is not an independent factor in our society, but is the natural result of changes in our time. More jobs are available to women, and with higher incomes. Financially it is more feasible for a woman to support herself and possibly a family. She may now choose to be single without concern for her survival.

It is becoming more socially acceptable to be single. Unmarried women sometimes have been seen as lacking status. A wedding band was evidence of some achievement. Today, it may appear as evidence of being trapped. However, being single or married is not a choice all women make for themselves. Though more boy babies are born than girls, by the age of marriage, there are more women than men, and some men choose not to marry. Therefore, some women will not marry. Women are widowed. Separation and divorce happen. There is not one pattern for the circumstances that bring women to the position of singleness.

We often visualize a single woman now as one who has shaken off the shackles of tradition. She is independent, free, self-sufficient, and possibly a swinger. A married woman may look at her single counterpart and envy her freedom to indulge in a wardrobe of her choosing rather than buying disposable diapers and formula. The unmarried woman may travel, take additional schooling, and order her own life-style. We see her as pursuing the profession of her choosing.

Singles bars reach out to the lonely person. Flashing lights, compelling music and the likelihood of meeting new companions beckon. One popular singles bar has two-hour long waiting lines of people wanting something to fill the empty hours.

Our society is accepting sex outside of marriage as a valid life-style, in sharp contrast to the words of Scripture that specifically say that sex apart from the commitment of marriage is wrong (Gal. 5:19; Eph. 5:3,5; 1 Cor. 6:9).

Books and magazines tell a woman how to make use of men without getting emotionally entangled or sacrificing any of her independence. Advertisements, TV programs, and movies glamorize immoral relationships. Economic, emotional, and spiritual independence are set as the ideal.

I listened recently as a group of single girls listed their problems: most at times felt lonely, were concerned about finances, and felt they lacked status. Some also had low self-esteem and wanted more companionship. They thought these problems were unique to them as singles.

Loneliness

Loneliness can be a severe problem for singles and one that God can help the person to handle. I watched a friend and business colleague wrestle with this. His second marriage had failed. He had been accustomed to coming home to lots of activity. Two preschool boys filled the house with clamor and variety. Now he entered a quiet apartment. Drapes were still closed as he'd left them. There was no clutter to step over, no noisy greeting. Ingenious decorating, carpeted walls and expensive sculptures did not crowd out loneliness. He connected a television to the light switch. Walking in the door would no longer be so overwhelmingly silent.

Many married people also experience loneliness. I asked several women whom they considered their best friend. Not one had a prompt answer. After a long pause, a few named their husbands. A surprising number did not consider their husbands as intimate friends. From the description of their relationships, the husbands sounded more like persons with whom their lives had become entangled, men they would not have married if they had known what they know now. Some would have married the same man, but would have done many things differently. One husband and wife never talk about their feelings. They have not been "one flesh" for over seven years. Each is lonely.

Needs

God created each woman. Because He has complete knowledge, He is aware of who will marry and who will remain single. He knows how long a woman will be married and all about the person she will marry. Knowing a woman will remain single does not prevent God from giving her emotional needs that usually are only fufilled in marriage. God's promises apply to every believer. When He says He will supply all our needs, this applies to the happily married, unhappily married, and the unmarried.

One of the greatest needs of any woman, of any person, is self-worth. In our society, a woman has traditionally been thought to gain worth through marriage. The single woman may feel that she has no significant place in a family-oriented society. However, the needs for self-worth are the same, for marrieds and unmarrieds, as well as the need to be needed and important to another.

God is the ultimate Giver of worth. The woman who is His child knows the Lord of hosts, the God of all the earth. She has been purchased by the Redeemer who knows her intimately. He is the Holy One of Israel, and His solutions to her problems will not be second best.

To understand worth in the light of Scripture and of personal relationship with our Father God leaves no room for low self-esteem. Each woman is wonderful because she has been made and claimed by a wonderful God. She can personally acknowledge this whether or not her feelings agree at the moment.

In Scripture, there are many names given to Christ—134 according to Cruden's Concordance. Some of them refer to His relationship to His people as a group. But many of them also refer to a personal, one-to-one kind of relationship in which He is Shepherd, Friend, Light, Saviour, Head over all things, Mediator, Deliverer, Everlasting Father, Bread of Life, Gift of God, King, Vine. Also, the Holy Spirit is called our Teacher, Comforter Guide. The work of the Spirit is personal to each individual as well as taking place in the world and in the church. Every woman can know within herself that God is ministering to her in terms of her personal needs, goals, outreach, and her relationships.

A single woman has a special opportunity to come to a deep understanding of self-worth since she is not able to lean on a husband for borrowed value. She needs to come to know who *she* is as a unique person. God can guide her in this search which will be centered in the Scriptures, just as mine was. The experience that she brings to her search may be different than that of a married woman, but the human qualities and longings are the same.

Ellen was a Christian but not a growing one. She became involved with a man. As a result of that relationship, she gave birth to twins. They lived only a few minutes. Ellen thought God could never use her because of that time of her life. But God is an economist. He has a purpose for each of us, Ellen included. As she grew spiritually, God gave her a Christian husband and children. God also gave her the special ability to encourage people during hard times. His love for her has been multiplied and shared.

Don't Play with Fire

Many people make "provision for the lust of the flesh" by searching for companionship in the wrong places. This is not only a problem for single people but also for married people who are dissatisfied with their mate. Two married people may be in the same room and still feel the ache of needs their mate cannot or will not meet. This void searches for something or someone to fill it.

When a Christian woman sets aside God's instruction and either through ignorance or deliberate disobedience gets involved with a man to whom she is not married, she is welcoming many problems. Some take effect immediately. Others surface later. For a Christian who dabbles with sin, an appetite is stimulated that grows.

Salvation isn't lost but the joy of salvation disappears. The relationship with God isn't broken; He never leaves us. But we no longer feel comfortable with Him. We can't enjoy His fellowship, and fellowship with His people becomes strained.

Living one thing and trying to be another causes conflict and inner tension. When we have confessed our sin and God has forgiven us, that old appetite is still there. Satan is a clever arranger of circumstances. Sights, songs, individuals arouse that appetite. How much better never to have let the appetite develop, never to give the devil that room.

God Forgives Guilt

Guilt is another tool in Satan's hands. He says, "God can't use a vessel like you. Your future is ruined." We have available the weapons we need for this kind of battle.

We are told repeatedly in Scripture that our acceptance to God is not based on our perfection. It if were, there would be no hope for any of us. Our position with God is due to Christ's sacrifice and our acceptance of that sacrifice. If you ever fear that you have lost your position with God, memorize a few verses such as Ephesians 2:4-6. "But God, being rich in mercy, because of His great love with which He loved us, even when we were dead in our transgressions, made us alive together with Christ (by grace you have been saved), and raised us up with Him, and seated us with Him in the heavenly places, in Christ Jesus." When Satan, the Accuser, speaks up, remind him of that truth.

You Need the Church

All believers need the companionship of a local church. It requires initiative for the single woman to search for other Christians and identify with them. I have a friend who did this. But then she expected them to make 100 percent of the effort to keep her company. It takes times and energy to develop meaningful relationships. Just as a husband and wife must spend time getting to know each other, so single people must spend time cultivating friendships.

It is of great value for singles to make friends with Christian families. Too often we segregate our body of believers into the "marrieds" and the "singles." What a shame. Both groups have so much to offer each other—and more in common than we often think. When we make that separation, both groups miss the blessing of seeing how God works in different circumstances. "Marrieds" think the "singles" have it made, that they are financially independent and don't have to make elaborate arrangements just to get away for a weekend.

Sometimes, the singles are seen as not being very involved in the weekly responsibilities and activities of the local church. Singles look at the marrieds and think they never experience loneliness, and therefore cannot relate to singles' problems in finding companionship. Often, the needs of singles aren't included in organizing church activities—which tend to become so family-centered that singles feel like fifth wheels. Every believer is given gifts which are profitable to the local body of believers (Rom. 12:5–6). We need each other.

Make room to be hospitable! Open your home or apartment for Bible studies, and other get-to-gethers. Give people a chance to get to know *you*. You may have to increase your grocery budget a little. But the investment will be worth it.

Unmarried people can have a definite ministry

with children. In return, the children will minister to them.

One single man spends his Sundays with several underprivileged boys. They worship together, eat at a carry-out spot, and play games and sports in a park. This man is helping close the gap where a father image is lacking. The boys learn love and respect for a godly man, making it easier for them to love the Lord as their heavenly Father.

One girl spends an occasional weekend with the children of friends so that the parents can get away together for a few days. In turn, they help her with heavy jobs at her home.

Children are excellent distractors. When Jesus called them to Himself, I can imagine Him delighting in their pats and giggles. He was probably refreshed by their literal observations and openness. Single people can be enriched by loving our children and being loved in return.

For some months, our family circle included a Christian brother whose marriage had stopped functioning. I thought our ministry would be in providing a home, meals, and ears to listen when he needed to talk. I learned that the main ministry of our home was not in relieving his financial burden or giving adult fellowship. What he needed was our children. After the emotional trauma of being pushed away from his wife and family, he needed little people to meet him after work, sticky hands to wave and call "Bye" as he left in the mornings. He needed the interruptions—little people crawling under the paper onto his lap pleading for him to play "log" (that means lying on the floor and getting rolled on as long as you can take it!).

We often don't know the backgrounds of people our lives touch. And even when we do, we may not know where they are hurting. We cannot help each other when we allow the barriers between us to remain. Segregating the "marrieds" and "singles" deprives everyone. It interferes with Jesus' objective for us, "that they may all be one" (John 17:21).

Plan for Singles

When Paul wrote to the church at Corinth, he talked about the matter of singleness and marriage. His conclusion was that the single person could give more undivided attention to God, and thus, it was a way of life with many blessings. "One who is unmarried is concerned about the things of the Lord, how he may please the Lord; but one who is married is concerned about the things of the world, how he may please his wife, and his interests are divided. And the woman who is unmarried, and the virgin, is concerned about the things of the Lord, that she may be holy both in body and spirit; but one who is married is concerned about the things of the world, how she may please her husband" (1 Cor. 7:32–34).

God's plan for singleness is to secure undistracted devotion to Himself. Paul continues, "And this I say for your own benefit; not to put a restraint upon you, but to promote what is seemly, and to secure undistracted devotion to the Lord" (1 Cor. 7:35).

Single Is Special

We have dramatic examples in Scripture of God's special love for single people. Five resurrections from the dead closely involved singles. Peter raised up Dorcas (Acts 9), Elijah raised up the widow's son (1 Kings 17), Jesus raised the son of the widow of Nain (Luke 7), Jesus raised up Lazarus, a single man and brother of Mary and Martha (John 11), and Mary Magdelene was the first to see Jesus after His resurrection (John 20).

When we think back to the Old Testament, we remember women like Naomi and Ruth, both of them widowed, who were chosen by God to enter into the family of David, and thus into the family of the Messiah. Or there was Miriam, the sister of Moses, who played a significant part in leading the people, and Esther, who was chosen to leave her singleness in order to be a redemptive person of God in a heathen palace. In the New Testament record, we think of Lydia, a seller of purple fabrics, who opened her home to be used as a church, and the four daughters of Philip the Evangelist, who were prophetesses.

Some of the most profound statements of Jesus were said to or about single people. When watching the people give their offerings in the temple, Jesus said to His disciples, "This poor widow put in more than all the contributors to the treasury; for they all put in out of their surplus, but she, out of her poverty, put in all she owned, all she had to live on" (Mark 12:43-44). Regarding the woman taken in adultery, Jesus said, "He who is without sin among you, let him be the first to throw a stone at her" (John 8:7). To the woman at the well, who after five marriages was again single, Jesus said, "Whoever drinks of the water that I shall give him shall never thirst; but the water that I shall give him shall become in him a well of water springing up to eternal life" (John 4:14). And also to her He said, "God is Spirit; and those who worship Him must worship in spirit and truth" (4:24).

A Home in Bethany

One family of three single adults was especially blessed by the presence and power of Christ. Mary, Martha, and Lazarus were sisters and brother who lived together. It was their privilege to host Jesus when He was in the area of Bethany. We are given some glimpses into their personalities. Martha was "in charge." The home was referred to as hers (Luke 10:38) and she was the one bustling around, worrying about the details of the household. Martha was outspoken and said what she felt.

Mary was more docile and was a learner. She sat at Jesus' feet and heard His Word (Luke 10:39). We are told nothing about Lazarus' personality. Perhaps it was submerged behind Martha's dominance. Often around her kind of personality, unless it is Spirit-controlled, it is easier to fade into the background than to risk locking horns.

We know that Jesus loved all three of them (John 11:5). When Lazarus was sick, his sisters sent for Jesus. Jesus delayed going, for purposes of His own, and during the delay, Lazarus died. It could have been that Mary and Martha doubted Jesus' love for them because He didn't rush in to solve their problem. However, in God's economy, the time was not wasted. Jesus was preparing an experience for Mary and Martha that would change them. He was substituting the good with the best, and it required time. Most of us don't really appreciate God tampering with our time schedules.

When Jesus arrived, Martha, the more assertive of the women, went out to meet Him. She confronted Him with the question that both she and Mary had, "Lord, if You had been here, my brother would not have died." And it was to Martha, the confronter, that Jesus made His great declaration

A Single Person / 155

of life and hope. "I am the Resurrection and the Life; he who believes in Me shall live even if he dies, and everyone who lives and believes in Me shall never die. Do you believe this?" (John 11:25–26)

Then, Jesus called for Mary to come to Him. Martha went home to tell Mary that Jesus wanted to see her. The comforters followed Mary but not Martha. Sometimes, we assume that the Martha types do not need comforting during crisis times, as do the Marys. This is not true. Both need our tenderness and compassion, and often the Marthas have so long borne responsibility, and perhaps hurts, with strength that they need our care even more than the Marys who find emotional release with every problem.

Mary and her friends came to Jesus, in their deep sorrow, and He was deeply moved, and asked where they had laid Lazarus. And then Jesus wept, thus entering fully into the sorrow of this family.

Along with the mourners, Jesus went to the tomb. He shared the sorrow of the family. He also shared in the purpose of God—so that Mary and Martha, and His disciples, might see the glory of God in the raising of Lazarus.

Jesus asked the people to roll the stone away. Some of them probably didn't feel like pushing it. But Jesus was preparing a faith-building experience for them. Do you have a problem you are expecting God to solve while you sit back and watch? Listen to Him. He may be telling you what *you* should *do* about the situation. He may want to give you a faith-building experience. But He is waiting till you are willing to obey Him.

They took the stone away, and Jesus thanked the Father. Lazarus hadn't come from the tomb, but

Jesus gave thanks anyway. Do we thank God for answering our prayers before we see the answers? Or do we want to see the solution first? "Be anxious for nothing, but in everything by prayer and supplication with thanksgiving let your requests be made known to God. And the peace of God, which surpasses all comprehension, shall guard your hearts and your minds in Christ Jesus" (Phil. 4:6-7).

Jesus called Lazarus by name and he came out of the tomb wrapped in his grave clothes. But who can function well when he is bound? When Jesus gives new life, the project isn't finished. Jesus wanted Lazarus to be loosed, to be free to move. Whether it be your past, your frustrated hopes, your less than perfect self, Jesus wants you to be free. There was something for Lazarus to do for Jesus—he was to let the neighbors see him walking, running, laughing. Why? "For the glory of God, that the Son of God might be glorified thereby" (John 11:4).

We have two other glimpses of this family. One was on the occasion when Martha was preparing supper and Mary was sitting at Jesus' feet listening to Him. Martha became bothered and asked the Lord if He didn't think Mary should help. His answer was, "Martha, Martha, you are worried and bothered about so many things; but only a few things are necessary, really only one, for Mary has chosen the good part, which shall not be taken away from her" (Luke 10:41–42).

The other picture of the three takes place in the home of Simon who hosted a supper for Jesus and His disciples in Bethany. Martha was serving, and Lazarus was one of those at the table with Jesus. His very existence was evidence of Jesus' power—enough evidence that the chief priests wanted to kill him (John 12:10). Mary took a bottle of expensive ointment and poured it on the feet of Jesus and then wiped them with her hair. Her simple act of love caused her to be remembered for all ages. Her act was criticized but Jesus defended her. "Let her alone, in order that she may keep it for the day of My burial. For the poor you always have with you; but you do not always have Me" (John 12:7-8).

A Unique Individuality

To be God's single woman, God's woman who perhaps is not single but lives with aloneness, will mean a unique individuality of experience as illustrated by the difference between Mary and Martha, between a Naomi and a Lydia, or Ruth and the woman at the well. Jesus knows each of us and ministers in personal ways to our needs.

To be God's single person often means living against the tide of society, even of church, or of friends. May I suggest some verses for you? I hope these will help you to become even more God's woman—assured, confident, thoroughly furnished to every good work.

Are you tempted by fear? "But now, thus says the Lord, your Creator, O—————(put in your name), and He who formed you, O—————'Do not fear, for I have redeemed you; I have called you by name; you are Mine!'" (Isa. 43:1)

Are you in a rut? Does your life seem stagnant? "Behold, I will do something new, now it will spring forth; will you not be aware of it? I will even make a roadway in the wilderness, rivers in the desert" (Isa. 43:19).

Perhaps you think the roadblocks in your life are large, the stone to roll is heavy. "I act and who can reverse it?" (Isa. 43:13) "Those who wait for the Lord will gain new strength; they will mount up with wings like eagles, they will run and not get tired, they will walk and not become weary" (Isa. 40:31).

Are there times when you feel overwhelmed? Pressures to which you are subject may be different from those of any of your friends. God knows and will make it possible for you to cope.

"I will not leave you comfortless, I will come to you" (John 14:18). "For God hath not given us the spirit of fear; but of power and of love and of a sound mind" (2 Tim. 1:7, KJV).

Has God called you to be single at this time in your life? Are you married but alone? Remember that you are God's special person. Give your time and energy to Him. "Faithful is He that calleth you, who also will do it" (1 Thes. 5:24, KJV).

12.
Who Is Equal?

Equal. What a confusing word. It has only five letters in it. Its definition in Webster's Dictionary takes up the same amount of room as most words. For many years *equal* meant a sign I used in math classes. It did not arouse my emotions at all. Now the word has taken on new significance.

I was in a neighbor's living room. Women's friendly chatter and the aroma of coffee filled the room. A congressional hopeful said, "I suppose you're wondering where I stand on the Equal . . ." The room became silent. I put my coffee cup down. Within three minutes the room was electric. Women were aligned in two opposing groups. My blood was racing. There was no more friendly chatter in the room that morning. The smiling young lawyer was no longer a good guy. He was either an arch foe or the only candidate with any logic.

The word *equal* has been at the center of millions of hours of court time. The amount of money spent on its behalf has probably not been computed. The federal government shelled out six million dollars for the National Women's Convention alone. *Equal* was probably the most used word there.

What Does "Equal" Mean?

The word is not used frequently in Scripture. There are only 16 references listed under *equal* in my concordance. As Bible scholars try to grapple with this word, many more personal opinions are floating around than "Thus saith the Lord." Our society now is trying to swallow the concept that everyone is equal. Men are equal to women. Women are equal to men. Rich equal poor. Poor equal rich. We see much evidence in Scripture that we are not all equal in the sense that the word is commonly used.

We use equal today in the sense of being exactly the same, interchangeable. We see from the parable of the talents that people are different (Matt. 25:14-30). We read Scriptures in which women are given different instructions than men. It seems that the emphasis on equality in our society today is to force one person to give another person the equivalent of what he or she has that is of worth. This may be job opportunity, income, social security checks, or hours of leisure.

Acquiring these "rights" is seen as a desirable objective regardless of the cost to the giver or the society at large.

Herein lies the conflict. The person possessing what is of worth does not want to let go of it, does not want to take the risk of giving it or sharing it with someone else. The result? Conflict over "rights" and equality, whether the setting be labor-management, husband-wife, employed-unemployed.

Who Is Equal? / 161

This strikes a clang of discord when we see Jesus willingly elevating people through serving them.

Paul, under Roman house arrest, wrote to the church at Philippi, and said, "Do nothing from selfishness or empty conceit, but with humility of mind let each of you regard one another as more important than himself; do not merely look out for your own personal interests, but also for the interests of others. Have this attitude in yourselves which was also in Christ Jesus, who, although He existed in the form of God, did not regard equality with God a thing to be grasped, but emptied Himself, taking the form of a bondservant" (Phil. 2:3–7).

If person served person and looked out for the interests of others there would be no need for demanding rights. Job administered justice to his slaves (Job 31:13) on the basis that God was the Maker of them both. Although Jew discriminated against Gentile, Jesus broke down the wall that separated them. Peter made this statement, "God has shown me that I should not call any man unholy or unclean" (Acts 10:28).

Snobbery between rich and poor should be nonexistent. "The rich and the poor have a common bond, the Lord is the Maker of them all" (Prov. 22:2). And "He who oppresses the poor reproaches his Maker, but he who is gracious to the needy honors Him" (Prov. 14:31).

We might well ask the same question that Malachi did. "Do we not all have one Father? Has not one God created us? Why do we deal treacherously each against his brother . . . ?" (Mal. 2:10)

Then how do we as Christians function with all our differences? How do we know who should do what since we are not all identical?

Some women want to be their husbands' equals. This results in a power struggle. Men either rebel against a woman pushing for her rights or abdicate their "maleness" and fade into the woodwork.

Do You Want a Role?

In Christian literature, much has been penned recently referring to "roles" of men and women. As I study women in Scripture, they often do not conform to the "roles" we have defined for the woman of today. In that case, we must conclude that the "roles" as we have structured them are either incomplete or incorrect.

Most role definitions for the Christian woman today include caring for the home, raising children, and assisting her husband. These are valid functions. But if we limit women to that, where does Priscilla the tentmaker fit in? What do we do with Mary and Martha? To our knowledge, they had no husbands and raised no children.

Perhaps we want to find a "role" for woman and a "role" for man because we are comfortable with structure. "Here is what I have to do and here is what I don't have to do. This is my job, that is yours." We find comfort in rules. I am reminded that the Children of Israel wanted a king (a human one.—see 1 Sam. 8:5, 19). They wanted someone to tell them what they could and could not do. This shows immaturity. God wanted them to look to Him for direction.

I see a parallel to this in our society. In our battle for social equality today, creativity is stifled. We want the comfort of a "role" to fill. It is easier to conform to procedures than to search God's mind for His individual direction.

Where we find specific instruction for women in Scripture we have one option: to obey. Where the Bible is not specific we have another option: freedom—with God's direction. We discover that freedom has two aspects. We are free "from" in order to be free "to." As we look at Scriptures related to women, let's not look with a confined mind. I believe we will find the function of woman allows unlimited room for spiritual growth toward real freedom.

Man and Woman

Man meaning "male and female" was created in the image of God. "And God said 'Let Us make man in our image according to Our likeness; and let *them* rule over the fish of the sea and over the birds of the sky and over the cattle and over all the earth and over every creeping thing that creeps on the earth'" (Gen. 1:26).

In my imagination I try to visualize what humankind would be like today if we had not rebelled against God. Our intelligence would be beyond any measuring instruments available today. Our creativity would never have permitted boredom. Our understanding of our Creator would be beyond what our minds can fathom today. And fellowship! That would be beyond description. I needn't merely dream. I can look forward to the future, because I will be like Him someday. That new improved version of Miriam will be even better than Eve!

It is a sad fact that sin is a part of humankind. And as a woman I am affected by that fact. Sin has bound both men and women. Yet when we are in Christ, positionally, we stand together before

God: "There is neither male nor female; for you are all one in Christ Jesus" (Gal. 3:28).

That certainly does not describe secular men and women today. They are not one, they are competing. The battle is national and personal. Women's groups battle for "rights." Within marriages, men and women battle for who will run the program. This was all suggested in Genesis 3.

God gave Adam one simple command in the Garden of Eden. He was told not to eat of the tree of knowledge of good and evil. Eve was not yet created when this direction was given to Adam. It seems like such a simple request but its importance was great. God was giving man a test: would he obey his Maker? Eve knew God's instruction and was the first to violate it. Adam participated but Eve initiated. We find the result in Genesis 3:14-24. "To the woman He said 'I will greatly multiply your pain in childbirth, in pain you shall bring forth children; yet your desire shall be for your husband, and he shall rule over you'" (v. 16).

Woman was the bearer of children. Because death resulted from disobeying God (Gen. 3:19) more children would need to be born. It is the usual experience of women that pregnancy has discomfort. Yes, it varies from woman to woman. However, bringing a child into the world is probably the hardest work in the fewest hours a woman experiences. For many it is the most painful. This would be necessary to "multiply, and fill the earth" (Gen. 1:28). Woman would still want her husband.

God did not curse woman or man. He cursed the serpent and the ground. God told the consequence of the wrong action but he did not curse his two companions.

"And he shall rule over you." This statement

Who Is Equal? / 165

declares the result of eating the fruit. It was not God's desire, it was simply the result.

We see through history that woman has been ruled by man in most cultures. The "ruling" has sometimes gone to the extreme of considering her a possession similar to a slave, animal, or perhaps a toy.

Where God has been allowed to influence a culture the status of women improves. The patriarchs reverenced their wives; Jesus ministered to men and women alike. But in this world women and men cannot stand together as equals or as one. Sin has prevented that. The nearest we will come to that beautiful unity is in the marriage of a Christian man and woman. Then there is potential for that unity.

Our position before God as Christian men and women is equal; our experiences in life are not. Why are we equal in position before God? (1) Because we were both made by Him (Job 31:15; Prov. 22:2; Gen. 1:27), and (2) because we were both redeemed by Christ and made one by Him (Rev. 5:9; Eph. 4:4).

We can better understand what it means to be redeemed if we visualize the slave trade of that day. To redeem a slave was to buy him and then release him. In this case he could never again be put up for sale on the slave block. *Redeem* means "to release or liberate by payment of a ransom." Jesus' blood was the payment for sin of both men and women. Accepting His payment makes me free positionally as a woman. It is not God's intention that I put myself back on the slave block. It is not His intention that any person or group put me there.

We find in Scripture some references to functional differences between men and women. First Peter 3:7 tells husbands to live with wives as with a weaker vessel. Man usually has more strength than woman.

Early in our marriage I was determined to keep up with my energetic, powerful husband. His list of "Things to do" on Saturday was impressive. We would both get in high gear and begin tackling our projects. By early afternoon my smile would limp a bit. By midafternoon my soul was crabby. By evening I was either on the verge of tears or ready for an argument.

We found some alternatives. I take time to "supervise." (That means sitting down and watching *him* work.) He suggests that I slow down when he senses my energy crisis coming on. We have more delightful evenings together that way.

What will happen when women compete with men athletically? In some sports there is fairly even competition. In others (as we are already seeing), the women lose and men walk off with the trophies. The advocates of ERA are not going to like that. But it will happen. Men and women are not identical.

In the Family

Many sections of Scripture with instruction for women refer to home and families. "Older women likewise are to be reverent in their behavior, not malicious gossips, nor enslaved to much wine, teaching what is good, that they may encourage the young women to love their husbands, to love their children, to be sensible, pure, workers at home, kind, being subject to their own husbands, that the Word of God not be dishonored" (Titus 2:3-5).

Who Is Equal? / 167

It is not an option for a married Christian woman to neglect her family and her home. She may be gainfully employed outside of her home, but she cannot allow that involvement to crowd family and home responsibilities out of her life. God cannot be honored by families and households in turmoil. So He gives guidelines for order in the family. Love is the ingredient cementing the relationships. Organization and work are the ingredients in keeping the home. All ingredients require, among other things, time.

Men are admonished to provide for their families. "But if any one does not provide for his own, and especially for those of his household, he has denied the faith, and is worse than an unbeliever" (1 Tim. 5:8).

God is not honored by a man who could work but doesn't. Man is not promised that providing for his family will be easy (Gen. 3:17–18). In fact, it is likely to be difficult. When the family is "provided for," the wants race ahead of the needs. Still, that task is part of his job description.

As woman is not excluded from the working world, man is not excluded from the sphere of influence in the home. He is to bring the children up in the discipline and instruction of the Lord (Eph. 6:4). This means he must know his children and have a good relationship with them. This requires more than love; it requires time.

In listing the qualifications for a church leader, we find this verse: "He must be one who manages his own household well, keeping his children under control with all dignity" (1 Tim. 3:4). If a man wants to fulfill that requirement, he must be involved at home.

We find differences in Scripture regarding the

function of men and women in the church: "A woman should learn quietly and humbly. Personally, I don't allow women to teach, nor do I ever put them in authority over men—I believe they should be quiet" (1 Tim. 2:11–12, PH). And, "An overseer, then, must be above reproach, the husband of one wife" (1 Tim. 3:2). Also, "Let the women keep silent in the churches; for they are not permitted to speak, but let them subject themselves, just as the Law also says. And if they desire to learn anything, let them ask their own husbands at home; for it is improper for a woman to speak in church" (1 Cor. 14:34–35).

The Pastor Is a Man

The pastor-teacher of a local body of believers is to be a man. It is a real possibility that in our generation, applications for pastors could not include designation of sex. That does not change God's Word. We are not surprised when the world ignores Scripture. That we are trying to rationalize away God's instructions within the body, however, is wrong.

Why is there such turmoil over the function of women in the church—whether she may or may not be a pastor-teacher? There are at least three reasons.

First, in our times, the women's movements are trying to wipe out any differences in treatment of men and women. Their objective is social equality. This is an area where Scripture differentiates between sexes; therefore, it is a target for attack.

Secondly, we are in a position-conscious, status-conscious era. Everyone wants to be in charge. Women are not excluded from the race. Our Lord

Who Is Equal? / 169

must be very sad to see the squabble over leadership positions. He faced it when the mother of James and John wanted her sons seated on either side of Him in His kingdom. In these days it is unpopular to serve. Few people would sign up to be foot-washers in the modern church.

Recently, I was on a panel with some pastors, to discuss "The Woman's Role in the Church." We were each to identify ourselves before the discussion. In their introductions, all of the pastors included the number of people in their congregations. It seemed that they felt part of their status came from how many people were under them. Each pastor also mentioned that there were few old people in his congregation. What a sad commentary on these churches!

Leading others is popular; serving others is not. We value an individual by how many followers he or she has. This is not God's measure of value. Our great desire should be to serve.

> But Jesus called them to Himself and said, "You know that the rulers of the Gentiles lord it over them, and their great men exercise authority over them. It is not so among you but whoever wishes to become great among you shall be your servant, and whoever wishes to be first among you shall be your slave; just as the Son of Man did not come to be served, but to serve, and to give His life a ransom for many" (Matt. 20:25–28).

A third reason for the furor over women becoming pastor-teachers is what I call the pendulum reaction. From my perspective, women have not been functioning as fully as we should have been. There is no question that women were considered inferior beings during some stages in history. This resulted in women not functioning as the intelligent, capable beings God created them to be. Men have sometimes expected that women serve by pouring coffee and slicing egg-salad sandwiches —and that's all. As women become more aware of their value to our Lord, it is natural to want to be a more vital part of the ministry of the body. The pendulum swing can result in overreacting and taking the task that is not assigned us, namely, that of being pastor-teacher of the local body of believers.

The Basis for Unity

We have looked at references in Scripture that refer to differences between men and women. It is intended that we function with our differences and in unity. Philippians 2:1-2 tell us the basis for our unity." If therefore there is any encouragement in Christ, if there is any consolation of love, if there is any fellowship of the Spirit, if any affection and compassion, make my joy complete by being of the same mind, maintaining the same love, united in spirit, intent on one purpose."

Our unity is based on: (1) the example and encouragement of Jesus' life, (2) the incentive of His love, (3) the Holy Spirit in us and (4) our sensitivity toward each other. Based on these four wonderful facts, we make room for our differences. We thrive and grow together, not in spite of our differences, but because of them.

What Can Women Do?

Let's look at some of the areas in which women can minister.

Women can teach. Titus 2:3-5 gives us that instruction. Women have not fulfilled that direction. Young women are not being taught to love their husbands and children. If this admonition were carried out we would not have the divorce and parent-child problems prevalent in Christian families today.

We can and must teach our children about our Lord. Ephesians 6:4 tells fathers to do this and women are helpers in that job. Some Christian men don't assume that responsibility—a negligence that they will explain to the Lord someday. In these cases, women must follow through on the discipline and nurture of the children. We see that Lois and Eunice, Timothy's grandmother and mother, were successful in grounding Timothy in the faith. In order for women to teach, they must first study and learn. One may say, "But where do I begin? My mother did not set an example of biblical scholarship for me. Where do I start?"

We have a teacher, the Holy Spirit. The Apostle John wrote of His work in our lives. "And as for you, the anointing [referring to Holy Spirit] which you received from Him abides in you, and you have no need for anyone to teach you; but as His anointing teaches you about all things, and is true and is not a lie, and just as it has taught you, you abide in Him" (1 John 2:27).

Read the Word, study, and depend on the Holy Spirit to be your teacher.

Women can pray publicly. "Therefore, I want the men in every place to pray, lifting up holy hands, without wrath and dissension. Likewise, I want women to adorn themselves with proper clothing, modestly and discreetly, not with braided hair and gold or pearls or costly garments; but rather by means of good works, as befits women making a claim to godliness" (1 Tim. 2:8-10).

Does the word *likewise* not mean "in a similar manner"? This would imply that women are to pray in the same way as the men with the additional direction that their appearance not draw attention to themselves. Pagan women of that time might weave contrasting braids into their hair and deck themselves with jewels and rich silks. Should a woman be converted and continue this custom, this would detract from her spiritual ministry. A woman was to be characterized by her good works, not by her wardrobe.

First Corinthians 11:5 gives instruction for the woman while praying or prophesying. "But every woman who has her head uncovered while praying or prophesying, disgraces her head; for she is one and the same with her whose head is shaved." The reason for this covering is to show that she is submitting herself to the authority of God and her husband (if she is married).

It has been proposed that Paul, in writing this passage, did not approve of women's participation but simply recognized that they were doing it. This could not be. Paul was characterized by boldness. He spoke out against sin with words that stung at times. He would not have told women how they were to pray in public if he knew it was wrong for them to do it in the first place.

Women can share their spiritual blessings and insights with men. In fact, we have many instances of men learning from women in Scripture. I quickly add that this is not to be in the context of a woman pastor-teacher. We have already established that God has not given woman that function. The circumstances under which men learn from women are varied.

David learned from Abigail. Her appeal to him in 1 Samuel 25 kept David from murder. "And blessed be your discernment, and blessed be you, who have kept me this day from bloodshed, and from avenging myself by my own hand" (1 Sam. 25:33).

Apollos learned from Priscilla. "But when Priscilla and Aquila heard him, they took him aside and explained to him the way of God more accurately" (Acts 18:26).

Abraham was told by God to listen to Sarah. How can we enjoy God's blessings and not share with them that the whole body be edified and praise the Lord? God expects women to function for His glory in a variety of circumstances.

Abigail

We have many examples of godly, bold women in Scripture. Women who are learning need not fear that God has nothing for them. Abigail (1 Sam. 25) was the wife of Nabal who was worthless, foolish, and selfish. What a life that must have been. By her own declaration, he was wicked. She was aware of God's working and power and knew that David was God's chosen man to be ruler over Israel. She spoke with wisdom from the Lord, and see how God intervened for her! Not only did He remove Nabal from her life, but Nabal's replacement was beyond comparison. She became David's wife.

Some may question her method of doing something behind her husband's back; however, she was acting in what she believed was his behalf. She was also working to prevent the next king of Israel from assuming his position with the blood of her husband on his hands. It is evident that God honored her motivation. We do not know what God will do. He may, and probably will, change us. He is also capable of changing our circumstances drastically.

Deborah

As a woman, I have learned much about God through studying Deborah. We read of this prophetess in Judges 4. She prophesied during a period when Israel was in bondage to Jabin, king of Canaan. It is interesting that Israel was in bondage in the land where God wanted them to be free. (Do we choose to stay bound when He wishes us free?) Deborah was God's woman of the hour.

Some might say that she should not have had that job because the job description for a judge included the requirement that he be an able *man* (Ex. 18:21). Well, the fact is that she fulfilled her job and God blessed the results. We see that she was married to Lapidoth. She not only knew what God wanted done, but she was bold enough to speak to issues. Interestingly enough, she was called on to remind Barak of a message God had given him requiring bravery, initiative, and faith. He was to lead an army against Sisera, the captain of Jabin's army. Barak's answer to her reminder was this: "If thou wilt go with me, then I will go: but if thou wilt not go with me, then I will not go" (Jud. 4:8, KJV).

We may marvel at Barak's lack of faith and denounce his willingness to be disobedient. But in his eyes he was facing 900 chariots of iron with only manpower. For 20 years his people had been oppressed by Jabin, and his memories of God's power were obviously fuzzy, if they existed at all. However, Barak saw in Deborah something of God's strength, for he was will to go to battle if she were with him.

Now Deborah could have answered, "Women don't go to battle. My husband will go in my place. It's a man's job." But she did not. She could have said, "I'll go, but I must have Lapidoth at my side as my protector." God was guiding her directly.

We must be careful that we do not take one of God's principles and make it a rule to which not even God can make an exception. Barak gave up his honor because of his lack of faith. A woman was the one before whom Sisera fell. I like Deborah's morning reveille the day of the battle. "Arise! For this is the day in which the Lord has given Sisera into your hands: Behold, the Lord has gone out before you" (Jud. 4:14). Try a modern day personalized version of that on your husband some morning!

The result is given in verse 24: "And the hand of the Children of Israel prospered" (KJV). After the victory Deborah gave praise to God and her motherhood extended to all Israel as the result of her faith. She leaves an admonition for me: "But let those who love Him be like the rising of the sun in its might" (Jud. 5:31). May my love for Him be a powerful catalyst for growth.

Who Is Equal?

Equal? The word loses its glamor and militant appeal as I examine it in the light of Scripture. To desire to be identical with man would deter me from being the woman God wants me to be.

Equality will never be an objective that demands my supreme effort, for I have been created as unique; as part of God's good creation, I have been redeemed by Christ at the highest possible price.

Rather, it is my portion of the heavenly calling (Heb. 3:1) that elicits my full dedication. For I am part of the "chosen race, a royal priesthood, a holy nation, a people for God's own possession" (1 Peter 2:9).

> Therefore, since we have so great a cloud of witnesses surrounding us, let us also lay aside every encumbrance, and the sin which so easily entangles us and let us run with endurance the race that is set before us, fixing our eyes on Jesus, the author and perfector of faith, who for the joy set before Him endured the cross, despising the shame, and has sat down at the right hand of the throne of God (Heb. 12:1–2).